TALES FROM THE TRENCHES

*The First World War Stories of Corporal Alexander Norman
2nd Battalion Essex Regiment*

As told to his daughter

Mary Cole

2014

First published 2014.

ISBN 978-1-291-96012-9

ACKNOWLEDGEMENTS

My thanks are due to Ian Hook, keeper of the Essex Regiment Museum, for the comment 'Essex men didn't leave diaries'. To Malcolm Brown, Imperial War Museum, for the Tommy Bickerton story. To family members, for their memories. To David G. Jones, for saving and scanning pictures. To Derek, Jon, Sally and Rob for their help with the computer. And to Nora Black, for preparing the book for publishing.

PILGRIMAGE

Last night I walked where Alec marched
Under the Walls of Wipers.
I looked out on a peaceful town
He looked out for snipers

I looked up at the Great Cloth Hall,
And the medieval gable
He saw only rubble and death
As he buried the telephone cable.

I saw an arch made up of names
Of those who have no known grave.
He saw them fall, those friends of his
For a country they tried to save.

Up to Arras, then down to Ypres
The Essex move forward and back
One more battle, then onward again,
On with shovel and pack.

The lines where they fought are well defined,
For any with eyes to see,
A cross marks the graveyards across the lands
For those that died and are free.

But those that were left still soldiered on
For three score years and ten
Though they grew old, they never forgot
The lads who were never men.

They tended those graves, year after year
Till age and their wounds had their say.
Old soldiers, you know, will never die –
They all just 'faded away.'

So, go on a pilgrimage, stand where they stood,
Under the walls of Wipers,
Remember them all, and pray to your God,
There will never again be snipers.

Mary Cole
In memory of Corporal Alec Norman of the Pompadours

CONTENTS

ALEXANDER NORMAN

ALEXANDER NORMAN WAS BORN ON JUNE 21, 1893 in West Ham and died on October 3, 1974. He was an ordinary man, but lived in an extraordinary age. When he was born the automobile was in its infancy and had to be preceded by a man walking and carrying a red flag. When he died men had stood on the moon and space flight had become routine.

As a young man he had tuned his early crystal set to hear Radio Station 2LO. As an old man he watched instant pictures being beamed across the world by satellite onto the television set in his living room. As a youth he read of the Mayflower sailing the Atlantic to America. As a septuagenarian he flew the Atlantic by jet plane to visit his grandchildren.

His 81 years covered the greatest age of change the world has known. His life overlapped that of his youngest grandson by 11 months. He was too young to hear Granddad tell his stories and his sister was born too late. So this book of 'Granddad's Stories' is dedicated to Jonathan and Sally and our grandson Alexander Ethan Pryce, who never heard them first hand.

The stories are written as and when they were remembered. They are not in chronological order. They are written in the same way as I heard them as a child. Some facts have been verified and background has been added, but they must always remain 'Granddad's Stories'.

Alec was born in London, the youngest of twelve, but when he was still young, most of his family moved to North Benfleet to live in the country. Here he learnt all the country skills of growing vegetables and preparing rabbits and chickens for the table. He took up running across ploughed fields to get to school in time. He, with his dog Duke, learnt to stalk people and get around quietly and unseen. His teacher would not let him sit the scholarship exam to get into Grammar school as his entry form was five minutes late, so his parents sent him to live with his sister in London for the last few years of his schooling. He learnt to dodge through the busy traffic and to find his way round the city by foot, to save the penny tram fare.

Alec when he enlisted in August 1914

When he left school, he returned to Essex and became a linesman
for the telegraph company. When it was obvious that war was on the
horizon, he joined up, not full of gung-ho enthusiasm for killing the
Hun, but knowing the job had to be done, and having worked out
that by volunteering he could ask to become a signaller, and use the
skills he had learnt at work. Although there was much talk of people
volunteering, many people quickly came to the conclusion that some
sort of conscription would be necessary. (see *The War Diaries of an Essex
Rector*[1]).

Most of the local North Benfleet lads who joined up and survived
were also those who had moved to the country from London. They had
developed the quick wit and quick reactions of the Londoner and the
survival skills of subsistence living in the country. This was to be vital
in their survival. Soon after enlistment the new Essex men were sent
to Stamford for training. (Possibly the Colchester Barracks was too
overcrowded to cope with the new intake.)

No arrangements had been made for accommodating them and, late
at night Alec and his group were told to bivouac in a small open park.
Some of the local people remonstrated that they did not want twenty or
so soldiers camping on their doorstep but they settled down quietly to
sleep the best they could. When they awoke next morning, they could
not see the grass for sleeping figures – several troop trains had come in,
and they had ALL been sent to sleep in the park.

Alec walked round the town, and bought a silver spoon marked
'Stamford' with the town's coat of arms. He decided that he would buy
one in every town he visited whilst in the army, but he was moved on
so often, that the only other one he bought was in Arras! After the war
a history of the Essex Regiment[2] was written by J. W. Burrows. Alec
and his friends ordered copies, and Alec marked certain incidents with
a cross or tick or a one or two word comment. These have been helpful
eighty years later in putting these stories together.

---

[1] A. Clark. Diary of Andrew Clark. Oxford: Bodleian Library, 1856-1922.
[2] J. W. Burrows. The Essex Regiment. Southend-on-Sea: John H. Burrows & Sons,
   1927.

CAP BADGES

ONE OF THE SOUVENIRS THAT Alec kept from the war was a wide black belt, which had a number of cap badges fixed to it. As a child I was fascinated by the collection. I asked him about them and he said that he had swopped them for Essex badges. This didn't seem right to me... How did he get enough badges to swop? I didn't dare question him, so I just accepted it face value. It was after he died that I had the badges mounted into a frame.

When I was researching for this book, I found the answer. One old soldier said that it became a craze to see how many different badges could be collected, obviously from hats found around the trenches. So each badge represented a man who had been killed. No wonder Alec told a white lie to me as a child.

THE RUN AROUND

WHEN ALEC JOINED THE 2nd Essex Battalion at the out break of war in 1914, he either met up with three friends he already knew, or he made friends with these men in training camp. These four were constantly together throughout the war in what some in authority felt was an unholy alliance. One, we know was John Crudington of Pitsea, but the names of the others remain a mystery. One of the things these lads had in common was athletic ability, all being capable runners and long jumpers in village sports before the war.

One of the training exercises in P. T. (Physical Training) in initial training in England was to be able to leap across a mess table, which would have been 30 ins high by three feet across.

To Alec and his friends this was a piece of cake, so for fun they tried to leap the table length-ways. The table would have been 8-10 feet long. They, being athletes, could do this with ease. Unfortunately this was seen by a rather sadistic Sergeant-Major, who at the next P. T. session lined up the whole company and ordered them to jump the table length-ways. The men were aghast. Some were so unfit that they had trouble jumping across, let alone the length of the table.

The Sergeant-Major quickly said: "If someone like Norman can do it, anyone can. Show them, Norman."

This put Alec in a quandary. He knew full well that there were only four of them that could do this with safety, and that the Sergeant-Major was looking for a reason to put them on a charge. He could not disobey the order.

Alec took his run up, and luck was with him. As he jumped one foot caught the edge of the table. To stop himself sliding the length of the table, he managed to get one hand down, and converted the jump into a beautiful cartwheel. He landed on his feet in front of the Sergeant-Major and a passing officer.

"Well, that's one way Sir." he said.

We don't know what the officer said, but the company was never asked to repeat the exercise! After this the four friends were almost certainly the bane of the Sergeant-Majors life. They would stick up for the underdog, and had the wit and humour to turn most things to their advantage.

It was not surprising that they were frequently on punishment. One punishment was a route march of about 10 miles with full kit. This kit weighed in the region of 60lb. Another punishment was to do ten or twelve miles at the double, which meant getting back within a certain time or facing another charge. On one occasion Alec and a mate had so upset the Sergeant-Major that he ordered the route march at the double, with full kit. This was no joke. The Sergeant-Major inspected the kit bags, told them the route to follow and sent them off.

They set off at a good pace, knowing full well it would kill them to keep it up. But what the Sergeant-Major didn't know was that there was a very useful haystack a mile away, just out of sight of the camp. As soon as they got there the kit bags were emptied and refilled with hay. They were then able to do the rest of the course at good cross country speed, and always visible to any passer by. On their way back they were able to get back to the haystack with time to have a rest and refill their haversacks with the missing kit.

At the prescribed time the Sergeant-Major stepped out of the mess to meet the exhausted and broken men on their return. At last he would have the last laugh.

To his amazement, in came the two lads, at the double, each in step, each carrying full kit and not even out of breath! When they stopped in front of him, Alec said: "That was a nice run. Would you like to come with us next time, Sir?" That was another thing they weren't asked to do again.

Marius' Mules was the name the Romans called their infantrymen, on account of the load they carried on the march. It is still so today.

According to *A Medal For Life*[1] by Leslie Wm Bills the W.W.I. soldier was expected to move up in fighting order into prepared trenches with steel helmet, rifle and bayonet, entrenching tool, two gas helmets, wire cutters, 220 rounds of ammunition, two sandbags, two Mills bombs, a regulation ground sheet, water bottle, haversack and field dressing. The weight carried by each man was in excess of 66lb. Alec Norman would have carried all of the above plus maps (still in our possession), Morse code tapper, tools and a roll of cable and signal flags. He would also carry iron rations and spare socks and other clothing.

Prize winners waiting to receive prizes, Military Sports Day, May 15 1915. Alec is circled

---

[1] L. W. Bills. Medal for Life: Biography of Captain William Leefe Robinson. Staplehurst: Spellmount Publishers Ltd, 1990.

THE POLE VAULT

Alec was born in a part of West Ham called the Tidal Basin. His parents, James and Elizabeth, were staunch members of the local Nonconformist Chapel and workers for The Band of Hope, a Christian Temperance movement. Most of the people in the neighbouring streets belonged to docker families.

The two great evils of the time were poverty and drink. Men would line up and stand for hours hoping to be taken on to work a day in the docks, as there was no such thing as regular employment there. There were no benefits either, so no work meant no pay and no pay meant no money for food. When the men did get work and money a great deal of it was spent in the local public house. Elizabeth would try to persuade them to forsake the 'Demon Drink' and 'sign the Pledge' not to drink alcohol. They often did, but their pledges rarely lasted if they had money in their pockets. Alec himself signed the Pledge aged twelve and never drank a drop except for medicinal purposes, and even then under duress.

James had originally been a cordwainer (shoemaker) but had given up to become a postman. This gave the family the advantage of a steady wage, which was put to good use. The local grocer used to make 'penny pokes', which were screws of paper, containing one teaspoonful of tea, sugar and condensed milk. If a father had worked that day, a poke would be bought to make the evening cup of tea.

James and Elizabeth ran a Sunday School Class for the young boys of the area. If they attended they would be invited home to listen to the reading of the weekly serial from the 'Boys Own Paper' and perhaps to have the treat of tea with the family. Alec must have listened to these stories from a young age, and as soon as he could read, he became an avid reader of the 'Boys Own Paper'.

One particular story fascinated Alec, as it was headed by a picture of the hero of the story leaping a stream, using a pole to help him. Alec had never seen pole vaulting before and he soon knew every line of the drawing. He had two burning ambitions: one was to pole vault like that; and the other to discover where the scene was and to visit it.

During training Alec was sent to Stamford in Lincolnshire. On some days the lads were sent out on training runs through the fens. Most of the time this was like running through the fields of North Benfleet. The one difference was that the fields were interspersed with draining ditches to run the water off the flat land. At one point they came to a stream which had to be crossed. Alec looked up and could hardly believe his eyes. There in front of him, was the scene that had haunted him for years. Every detail was correct: it had to be where the illustration was drawn. Alec decided that he would return at the first opportunity with a camera, to record it for his friends and family.

He made a careful note of his bearings, but even with the aid of maps, he could never find the spot again.

THE GRAND OLD DUKE OF YORK

In November or December 1914 Alec was sent to Dover to embark for France. The detachment was sent to the army, barracks at the top of Castle Hill. In the morning they were marched with full kit (about 60lbs plus rifle) down to the docks. They waited all day in the freezing cold, only to find that as soon as it was dark they were ordered to march back up the hill again. The next morning they set off once more. Again they marched down the hill, only to wait and then be ordered back to barracks. This was repeated daily, with the morning march down the hill and the return journey after dark. The men were convinced that this procedure was somehow to convince the Germans that England had unlimited troops at its disposal.

In the end they embarked for France. As Alec said to his mates: "If they marched us up and down that hill much more, they'd have to change our name from Essex to The Duke of York's."

Forty years later Brian, Alec's eldest grandson, won a scholarship to the army school. It's name? The Duke of York's. Where was it? Beside the barracks at the top of Castle Hill, Dover.

Brian, centre front, the Duke of York's Field Day

Alec and his horseshoe

THE HORSESHOE

Soon after Alec arrived in France, he was stationed at Battalion H.Q. With the others, he had to take his turn at sentry duty in the street outside. He was not allowed to move from the spot, and had to remain at attention, except when challenging someone or saluting officers.

While standing there he heard a whooshing noise and then a crash on the wall beside him. This was followed by a clattering in the street. He could not leave his post to find out what had made the noise and could not even turn his head in that direction. A Tommy was coming up the street and had seen what had happened. He stooped down and picked something up from the pavement in a handkerchief.

As he passed Alec he dropped it at his feet, and out of the side of his mouth said: "With luck like that, you'll never die in France, mate," and was gone.

When he was at last relieved, Alec was able to pick up the offering. It was a now cooling horseshoe. In the wall, by the door he was guarding was a hole gouged out as the horseshoe had bounced around the back of his head. All Alec had to say was that Jerry must be in a bad way, if they were firing red-hot horseshoes instead of shells!

Alec carried his horseshoe around with him for luck for some time, but it was eventually left behind as his pack became too heavy.

In the 1960's Alec and the remains of the boys made a trip back to France, and he jokingly told the story. The lads quickly said "Lets go and see if it is still there."

Alec lead them up a side street, and there in the doorway was the hole, untouched after nearly fifty years. He had his photo taken at the spot and proudly told us about it. The only thing he didn't say was which town or village it was in.

I have been looking for it ever since!

SHELLSHOCK

The platoon had been led into sap which was at right angles to their trench. The Sergeant stood up to describe to the men what lay ahead of them and to show them the objective that they had been ordered to take when they were to advance. He faced No Man's Land while the men faced him and the rear of the trench.

Suddenly Alec shouted: "Down" and dived face down into the mud at the bottom of the trench. He was followed by all the men, who piled on top of him, with the Sergeant on top.

Moments later their world shook as a shell buried itself in the wall of the trench behind them and exploded. A second later and the whole platoon would have been killed.

When the Sergeant picked himself up, he said to Alec: "How did you know that one was coming?"

"I saw it in your eyes, Sarge" was the reply. With his extremely good eyesight he had seen a dot in each of the Sergeant's eyes, and with his quick reactions, had not only seen that they were getting larger, but that it could only have been a shell coming straight at them!

Contributed by Elsie Norman and Beryl Cole.

Afterwards Alec always said that the most important thing to do after a shell burst was to check the people around you.

If there was a pile of earth thrown up there was always a chance that your friends were under it. You needed to dive in and dig like mad at where you thought a friends head might be. If you found a leg, you went to the other end of the pile and dug there. The most important thing was to clear an airway and get the victim breathing again. He felt that too many lives were lost as men were suffocated while people wondered what to do.

I wonder how many men owed their lives to his quick thinking.

OBEYING ORDERS

To a messenger or member of the Cycle Corps, his bicycle was as important piece of equipment as his rifle, and, as with his rifle, it must never be out of his sight. The signallers and other ranks at Headquarters always respected this, for they knew that, even off duty, a messenger might be called on at a moments notice to deliver urgent messages.

Junior officers however had different views. Some young and inexperienced members of Headquarters staff could see no reason why they should not order a messenger to hand over his machine so that he might be spared the mile or so walk to the village bar in the evening.

On one occasion a messenger was ordered to make his machine available for an officers use at six o'clock. The man protested, but to no avail. He was given a direct order to leave his bike at a certain spot opposite the Officers Mess. At some time in the afternoon a new draft arrived, and as there was not enough room for them in the huts, a row of bell tents were erected, just in front of the Officers Mess.

Six o'clock came and the young officer arrived to take charge of his 'borrowed' bike. When he could not see it, he sent for the messenger, who claimed in an aggrieved tone: "But I left it where you said sir!"

By this time a group of officers had come out of the mess to see what the fuss was. The officer looked again, and saw the bicycle, strung up to the top of a bell tents guy ropes! There it stayed until the tent was lowered the next day.

As Alec said, "I can't think how it got up there!" but his eyes twinkled as he said it! And what was more, an order went out that bikes were not to be borrowed by anyone.

RATIONS

NAPOLEON SAID THAT AN ARMY MARCHES on its stomach, but one of the problems of the First World War was the logistics of the delivery and distribution of food to the men. If they were in the trenches and under fire, the rations would often not get through, while if they were in reserve, the cooked meals were served on a first come, first served basis, usually with supplies running out before the end of the queue.

When rations were delivered, the batman would insist on taking sufficient for the Officers, then the N.C.O.s would help themselves, and what was left would be divided according to the whim of the first man on the scene. Alec quickly realised this was causing friction between the men, and friction they could not afford. When the rations came up for the platoon that day he insisted that it was his turn to share them out.

He found that there were ten tins of bully beef between twenty of them, so he told each to get a partner. Then he made ten piles of food.

Each pile had one tin of Bully, then he cut each of the five loaves of bread in halves, one for each pile. Then he went round with the vegetables, which were not so easy, as they were all different, but each pile had approximately the same amount, although one might have an onion whilst another would have a parsnip. At last the job was done to his satisfaction.

The boys watched to see what would happen next. "Each pair can choose one pile of food, but in future whoever shares out the food will have the last choice. That means whoever does the job will have to be as fair as possible."

He then stood back till the others had chosen their food, and took the pile that was left. After this no-one ever dared to try to take more than their fair share of rations, and other units began to work on a fair-share-for-all system.

This was probably one of the reasons for the high morale of the Essex who always did stick together.

LIST OF ARMY RATIONS

For each man each day:-

Meat (usually bully or corned beef)	1 lb
Bread or dry biscuit	1 lb 4 oz
Bacon	4 oz
Tea	½ oz
Sugar	2 oz
Jam (usually plum and apple)	2 oz
Cheese	1 oz
Butter	¾ oz
Potatoes and vegetables	1 lb
Salt	1 oz
Pepper	1/36 oz
Mustard	1/20 oz

If these rations had been issued each day, they would have been boring, but adequate.

In some cases it would have been a better diet than they were used to. Unfortunately, in the trenches, these rations rarely arrived on time or in their entirety.

OBSERVATION POST

ALEC REACHED THE OLD BARN WITHOUT too much difficulty. It was a good thing he had taught himself to Indian crawl in those boyhood days at North Benfleet. No-one else could have got there without being seen. He was right, there was no hope of rigging a telephone wire across those shell holes in full sight of enemy snipers. The officer was right, it was an ideal observation post. He drew out his signal flags; he could observe the enemy through the gaping hole in one end of the barn, and signal back through the other.

Having reported back, Alec looked round the remains of the barn. It was obvious with the shell holes all around that it would not remain habitable for long. As he poked around in the rubbish, he found a strange hoard. Box after box of candles. He wondered who had acquired them and how they came to be in the barn. It was quite clear that nobody would come back to claim them at this stage of the war. As he pondered this, he heard a muffled squawking noise, and out from behind the boxes stepped a very disgruntled hen.

Now it was obvious to Alec that this hen would not survive, and its legal owner was either dead or many miles away. It was also obvious to Alec that he and his friends had not eaten chicken for a long time, and he was extremely hungry. In a very short time the chicken was dispatched and had become four chicken joints, each roasting over a circle of lighted candles. Alec stayed there all day, observing, reporting back by signal flag while turning his precious chicken joints.

The officer sent a message back telling him to retire, but Alec claimed he was still quite safe. No way would he leave before his chicken was cooked. The evening bombardment started and still Alec stayed at his post. At last his chicken was cooked. He hastily ate his share and made his last observation. He signalled back to the trench and, as the shells got closer, the officer sent back the direct order to return to base.

Alec grabbed the other pieces of chicken and stuffed them into his pockets. He blew out the candles and left hurriedly. He eased himself back along the trench, hearing the crumps as the shells got closer.

At last he got back to the dugout to make his report. The officer was overjoyed to see him back. "Come and sit with me", he said, "You deserve a medal for sticking to your post for so long. Tell me all about it."

Now the last thing Alec wanted to do was to sit near the officer with hot chicken in his pockets! He sat, keeping as much space as possible between him and the officer. He could hardly tell him the real reason for sticking to his post so bravely. Whether the officer felt the heat from the chicken and guessed what he had been doing, Alec never knew, but he never did get the medal! His friends never forgot that unexpected supper of chicken though.

Since Napoleonic times the British Army has provided rations (of some kind) for its troops, outlawing looting the land and all "acquired" food has to be accounted for so that reparations can be made. Some Essex lads found a pig in the ruins of a farm and brought it back to the trenches savouring roast pork for dinner. The self righteous Sergeant confiscated it declaring it to be 'derelict' and took it to the officer of the day. The officer also fancied fresh pork and insisted that it should be sent to Headquarters for 'evaluation'. The pig was dispatched and the only satisfaction that the men had was that the Sergeant didn't get his share either!

As Alec explained, if the lad had brought the pig in dead, they could have eaten it, as there would have been no chance of returning it to it's rightful owner. After that any chicken, rabbit or pig was always 'found dead' even if it had the appearance of being freshly killed!

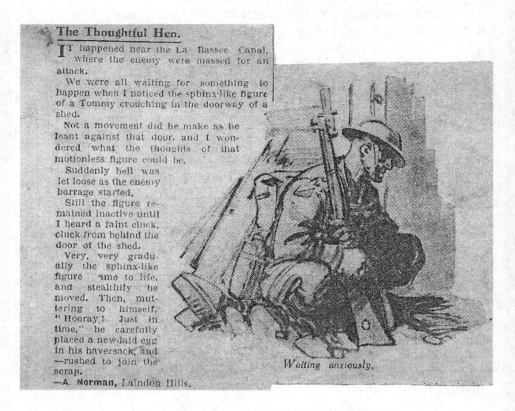

The Thoughtful Hen.

IT happened near the La Bassee Canal, where the enemy were massed for an attack.

We were all waiting for something to happen when I noticed the sphinx-like figure of a Tommy crouching in the doorway of a shed.

Not a movement did he make as he leant against that door, and I wondered what the thoughts of that motionless figure could be.

Suddenly hell was let loose as the enemy barrage started.

Still the figure remained inactive until I heard a faint cluck, cluck from behind the door of the shed.

Very, very gradually the sphinx-like figure came to life, and stealthily he moved. Then, muttering to himself, "Hooray! Just in time," he carefully placed a new-laid egg in his haversack, and —rushed to join the scrap.

—A. Norman, Laindon Hills.

Waiting anxiously.

'The reluctant hen! This is a story that Alec wrote and had printed in a national paper in the 1920s. We don't know whether it was an entrance to a competition, or something he saw in the war years, but he kept the cutting safely for sixty years. It is possible that the 'chicken in the barn' incident was also in the La Bassee Canal area.

ANOTHER OBSERVATION

AT THE TURN OF THE CORNER OF the trench that Alec's platoon was in stood a dilapidated old farm cottage, long since abandoned by its owner and long since used as a target practice by the enemy. Everyone was warned that across No Man's Land a sniper had his rifle trained on the building and that it would be fool hardy to even raise one's head. This condition of stalemate existed until a very new and very young Scottish officer arrived. He took one look at the remains of the sloping roof and said: "Why isn't there an observer up there? It would make an ideal spot."

Alec replied, "Yes, Sir, it would, but Jerry has seen it as well and has a gun trained on it."

"Don't be ridiculous, I want a volunteer to get up there and see what is going on." No-one offered their services. "Right then, I'll climb up there myself, just to show there's nothing to fear."

"I wouldn't if I were you, Sir," said Alec," you'll only get shot."

"Don't argue, I'm going up." And with that the officer climbed out of the trench to begin his assault on the roof. As he did so he looked back into the trench, only to see Alec standing, legs braced and arms stretched out.

"Why are you standing like that, man?" asked the officer.

"To break your fall and catch you when the sniper hits you, Sir" said Alec politely.

With that there was the crack of a rifle shot and the officer tumbled back into the trench, straight into Alec's arms and found himself very relieved to be still alive. Alec gently set him on his feet and, with very great restraint, said nothing. The officer, however expressed his thoughts forcefully. As Alec later said: "I didn't know the Scots had so many swear words!" The officer had learned that discretion was the better part of valour, and in that trench it meant keeping your head down.

According to the Second Essex Battalion History, on April 8th 1915, Major G.C. Binsteed was killed whilst looking out of the observation hole half way up the back wall of Central Farm.

OL' BILL

ONE OF THE THINGS THAT MADE LIFE worth living for Alec and the Essex boys was the humour of Bruce Bairnsfather. He was a Lieutenant in the Warwickshire Regiment who, having experienced the mud and slime of the trenches, started to draw caricatures of men and their humorous comments when he was holed up in a farm by the Douve River. Today these murals, done in a charcoal wash, on the plaster wall of the farm, would be thought to be priceless, but alas, within days of execution the walls became one more pile of rubble. Fortunately Bairnsfather copied them and, seeing an old copy of 'The Bystander' lying around, sent a sketch into them. They printed it and commissioned more so 'Fragments From France' and 'Ol' Bill' were born. These have recently been reprinted.

Alec had two favourites. One was of two Tommies, up to their waists in water in a shell hole, and one says to the other:-

"If you knows a better hole, go to it!"

The other was of a young soldier, pointing to a large shell hole in a wall and saying to a more experienced one:

"What made that?"

And the laconic reply:-"Mice."

These two jokes were repeated constantly for years until they became part of our childhood vocabulary. Even today if someone says:-"What made that hole?" the automatic reply would be "Mice". It was strange to find a reprint of these jokes in a Battlefield book shop, and after fifty years read 'Ol' Bill' myself.

On reading Bairnsfather's own account in *Bullets and Billets*[1] and the modern account in *Fields of Death*[2] by Slowe and Woods, it would appear that Bairnsfather got his 'Blighty One' (the wound that got him sent home) on 24th April 1915, and from the description of the area, the location must have been 'Oblong Farm' as this was within firing range of the Germans in Kitchener's Wood. The ironic thing was that at this time the Essex boys were on their way to relieve 'Mousetrap Farm', the more tactful name given to the originally named 'Shell-trap Farm' which was only a few hundred yards away.

---

[1] B. Bairnsfather. Bullets and Billets. London: Grant Richards, 1916.
[2] P. Slowe & R. Woods. Fields of Death: battle scenes of the First World War. London: R. Hale, 1986.

MOUSETRAP FARM

IN FACT THE ESSEX BOYS ARRIVED in the Wieltje area on the 30th April 1915, having been in the line in the Le Touquet area. On 2nd of May they had to withdraw owing to the Germans use of Chlorine gas for the third time. A party of 'A' Company managed to hang on until 'B' Company were able to give them some support.

It was decided to shorten the front line from six miles to three as it was over extended, and in places the front line was only ten yards from the enemy. The Essex had sustained 265 casualties, many of whom were gassed. During the retreat they were unmolested by the enemy, who were busy winning Hill 60 with another gas attack. From May 2nd to 10th the Essex were hammered by high explosive shell.

Brigadier-General Anley wrote: "The Germans seemed to rely solely on hammering their way through with heavy artillery. Although most of the men who were not wounded were dazed and bruised through being constantly buried, their fighting spirit did not appear to deteriorate. I heard of no men straggling to the rear. Each time the enemy's infantry tried to advance the men cheered and shouted to them to come on."

After a days rest in bivouacs in the reserve trenches the Essex relieved the Hampshire's in the support trench near Wieltje.

Shelltrap Farm was at a strategic position where two roads met before running into Ypres. It was held, on the 13th May, by an infantry company who had to retire after a three hour bombardment. This would leave a gap. It was important that the farm be retaken.

'C' Company accomplished this, with the aid of a machine gun, jumping into the moat and driving the Germans out. They desperately needed support. They got it:-

"...at 8.30 am the attack, carried out by the three remaining companies, started, being marked by the great boldness and determination; as the Essex passed the Rifle Brigade, the men of the latter jumped up in their trenches and cheered to the echo, a truly inspiring spectacle. Advancing in quick time, swept by high explosive and shrapnel, the companies topped a slight ridge where machine gun fire opened on them. Pressing on resolutely without a check they arrived within about 300 yards of the trenches, when with a roar the whole attack broke simultaneously into a double and charged home." [2]

Remembering that Alec and his friends were cross country runners, one wonders whose idea it was. If they knew that 'Ol' Bill's' originator had been wounded there, it would have been a grudge match!

---

[1] B. Brice. The Battle Booke of Ypres: A Reference to Military Operations in the Ypres Salient 1914-18. London: J. Murray, 1927.

FINDING THE RANGE

ONE OF THE FOUR FRIENDS was John Crudington of Pitsea. Possibly he, too, was a signaller.

On one day he and Alec were walking along the top of a trench, probably looking for a break in the telephone line, when a sniper opened fire. Crudington wanted to take cover as was prudent, but Alec insisted on keeping up a steady pace.

"If we keep on walking they will think we are out of range!"

They kept up a steady pace, with Alec giving a running commentary as to where the bullets were landing.

"That one was two yards in front of us!"

"That one fell short!"

"That one was too far to the right!

They walked on for some time with Alec keeping up his endless patter.

Then he said:-"Where did that one go? I didn't see what happened to it. It must have been fairly close."

"Too darned close," replied Crudington, "it went through my sleeve!" After that they decided to take a more sheltered way back!

Alec gained a reputation for being a 'lucky' type. Men and boys gained confidence from being with him. If he dived for cover into a shell hole, any of the boys who were nearby would jump in after him. If he decided to vacate a hole as being 'too hot' or too crowded, it would soon be vacated by all the rest. Whether he was 'lucky' or whether he used his skills and observations, we do not know, but one photo he took on a visit in the 1960s is of a particular grave in Gonnehem British Cemetery. It is of Private Arthur Pennell, aged 21 who was killed on 28th July 1918.

On the back of the copy he sent he sent to his daughter in America, Alec had written: "The only one who was killed when he was out with me."

TIN HATS

AFTER HE LEFT SCHOOL ALEC JOINED the G.P.O. as a telephone linesman. This involved climbing newly erected poles to 'lay the lines' to join people to this newfangled system of communication. Alec had joined up early in order to get the chance to be a signaller.

A signaller was not the same as being a linesman. Instead of climbing poles, he had to bury the line under the mud or pin it to the walls of trenches. He had to become proficient in both the Morse and Semaphore codes. He had to be able to strip, reassemble and use a Morse tapper and be able to take down messages sent in the same way. But the worst job was mending the line. Whenever a shell broke the wire, someone had to go out, follow the line to the break, search for the other end, splice a new piece of wire into the gap and then test that the line was working.

When he first went into the line, tin hats were unknown. When the first issue arrived, the Sergeant-Major was delighted. The hats were bare metal and nice and shiny. Here was something else for all the ranks to spit and polish, along with brass buttons and so on. Then came a bright and sunny day when the telephone line broke. Somebody had to go out and mend it. The first pair donned their tin hats and set off. Before long they were back, slightly injured by an unseen sniper. The line still had to be repaired. Another pair set off but were soon back with the same injuries.

Then Alec and his partner set out. Crouching, they made their way along the trench. But as they came to a shallower part, although they kept their heads well down, the sniper took a pot shot at them.

Alec looked at the bright sun and at his mate's tin hat. "Get that hat off" he said. Then he took off his own and daubed both hats with mud from the nearest puddle. The sun quickly dried the mud to a nice dull khaki colour. They put the hats back on and carried on down the trench. No more shots were fired. Their hats were no longer signalling their position to the enemy. They found the break in the wire, repaired it and tested it and set out on the return journey. They got back, expecting praise for using their initiative.

Did they get it?

No.

When the Sergeant Major met them, he took one look at them, and put them on a charge for having dirty equipment! A few months later camouflaged tin hats were issued to all ranks, but Alec never got any credit for their invention. Of course, this spontaneous adaptation probably happened up and down the line. There may even have been units where the officers thought of it.

Steel helmets were first issued in late 1915 and were not standard until 1916. Coppard's *With a Machine Gun to Cambrai* notes[1]: "An order was issued March–April 1915 abolishing the cleaning of buttons... Every piece of brass had to be dulled like gun-metal... to prevent the glint in the sunlight. This order was rescinded in August 1915. This secret order was issued by Major Stenhouse, a Staff Officer of 31st Division (Major S.B.L. Jacks)."

According to Peter H. Liddle[2] the 2nd Essex had a 2" red diamond to be sewn on sacking covering the steel helmet. The sacking prevented the helmets from reflecting light and it also softened then sharp outline of the helmet.

---

[1] G. Coppard. With a Machine Gun to Cambrai. London: HMSO, 1969.
[2] P. Liddle. The Soldier's War. Barnsley: Pen and Sword Books, 2010.

THE BATTLE OF THE SOMME

THE FIRST BATTLE OF THE SOMME commenced on July 1st 1916. The Battalion history[1] entitles the chapter 'A Trying Day'. Alec and the Essex boys arrived at the small village of Bertrancourt on the 12th of June, the vanguard spending the day laying cables. A fortnight was spent in training. It is clear that the Germans knew where they were, and possibly that an attack was coming as they started shelling Bertrancourt Cross Roads on the 28th, the day before the proposed action. Orders were given for a 48 hour postponement and the Battalion assembled at 11.30pm on 30th June.

The aim for this sector was to storm the villages of Gommecourt, Serre, Beaumont-Hamel and Thiepval. The Essex men were in between the Lancashires and the Newfoundlanders who perished at Beaumont-Hamel. The Essex were to aim for Pendant Copse and the church spire of Miraumont, which was beyond Puisieux Ridge. Between them and their objective was the fortification known as the 'Quadrilateral'. This was a system of deep trenches in which the enemy could take shelter during the initial bombardment. It looked straight down the hill to where the Essex boys were lining up!

The night before, pioneers were sent out with stakes and tapes, to mark the route the men were to take, which must have given the German machine gunners a perfect marker for the sights of their guns.

The Battalion left the jumping off trench at 8.36am, one hour after the barrage had lifted and nine hours after they had been assembled. They were in the third or fourth wave, following three battalions of 11th Brigade. They immediately encountered heavy artillery and machine gun fire, but made their way through the Quadrilateral and took Munich trench. However, they were driven back as they ran out of ammunition, the bearers being unable to get through to supply them. From 2pm to midnight they held the quadrilateral, when our own artillery started to shell it. Fortunately, a signaller (we don't know who) managed to signal with an 'electric lamp' or torch which had been found, and the barrage was stopped for long enough for them to retire. Soon after midnight they were relieved and found themselves back where they had started.

• 24 Officer and 606 Other Ranks went into action.

• 2 Officer and 192 Other Ranks survived.

• 22 Officers and 414 Other Ranks were gazetted as Killed, Wounded or Missing.

Although some may have been returned later, 949 have 'No known grave' and are commemorated on the Thiepval Memorial. By noon the next day the Essex were again in the same trenches, where they suffered another twenty casualties.

Alec makes no comment on the Regimental History's pages describing this day, but he and the boys always went back to the Thiepval Memorial and to the Beaumont-Hamel Memorial to the Newfoundland boys every time they visited France. For all my childhood we had a model of the Caribou memorial on the mantelpiece. The Memorial now belongs to the Canadian people. Newfoundland lost so many of its men at the Somme and other battles that it was no longer a viable country, and in 1949 became part of Canada.

Munich Trench is today the name of a small cemetery not far from Beaumont-Hamel. From it, looking right and left, can be seen the line of 1st July 1916, marked every few hundred yards by another cemetery, with its 'Cross of Sacrifice' shining in the sun. In front of the trench, on the next incline can be seen the copse, and from there can be seen the church spire. An unrealistic target to give the men. Even today this would be a long walk for those not encumbered with equipment, and with no enemy trenches to cross, let alone bullets and shells to avoid. Looking back from Munich Trench you can share the view the Germans had. Right into the Essex Camp!

---

[1] J. W. Burrows. The Essex Regiment. Southend-on-Sea: John H. Burrows & Sons, 1927

The Caribou memorial to the Newfoundland men at Beaumont–Hamel.

Letter of the Day

Hussar for the loyal Tsar!

AT THE end of the first day of the Somme, my father-in-law was one of 170 survivors out of 800 in the 2nd Essex. But for the actions of the Tsar, it could have been much worse. Responding to a plea from General Haig, the Tsar authorised a diversion: General Brusilov launched the Army of the Ukraine in a surprise attack which swept through the German lines. In a panic, the Germans withdrew 15 divisions held in reserve behind the Somme front. But for the Russians, the disaster of July 1916 could have been greater.

In the end, the Brusilov Offensive cost a million casualties. The Tsar paid for it with his throne and his life. Our historian Liddell Hart comments that whatever happened during and after the Revolution, not for the first time had the Russians come to our aid.

Certainly my father-in-law may owe his life and my family its existence to Nicholas II and the Russian soldiers who sacrificed themselves for their allies. As the Imperial Funeral unfolds, we should remember those million Russians — and the Tsar who never let his allies down.

Derek J Cole,
St Leonards on Sea, Sussex

TSAR NICHOLAS: Unlikely saviour of the Somme

The 2nd Essex were remembered in the Express on the Day of the Tsar's Funeral on 18th July 1998, 82 years later.

36

YOU FOUR

IT HAD BEEN A HORRENDOUS DAY. The Battalion had been ordered to advance, but it was hopeless. No sooner had they left the trenches, the enemy machine guns and artillery had opened fire. Men were cut down in swathes. There was no defence. The lucky few dropped into shell holes that offered meagre protection. Alec was one of them. His rifle was puny defence against the bombardment from the target trenches.

He did what he could for those around him, but that was little. Most were dead or dying. There was no way he could advance or even retire. There were no living officers or N.C.Os to give orders. The only thing to do was to keep his head down until it was dark enough to return to the jumping off trench. When he eventually regained its relative safety, he found that his three friends had also managed to crawl back.

They looked for other survivors and when they didn't find any, made their way back to the rear where the reserve was held. As they stumbled in, overcome by what had happened to their mates, and hardly believing they were still alive, they were met by the Sergeant-Major, who had tears running down his face. He said "I've lost a whole Company of good men today. Only you four made it back. And you were the four I could have done without." They always knew the Sergeant-Major didn't like them!

According to the Regimental History, an attack was made on the Le Transloy line in October 1916. One Company had four survivors and another had twelve who returned to the trenches by 9pm. The Battalion had 255 casualties: 14 killed, 75 wounded and 166 missing. Many of the missing were later reported killed. A few returned the next day. Whether or not this was the occasion referred to by Alec, we can't prove, but the strange thing is that it is one of the few incidents which is not marked with a tick or a cross in the margin of his copy of the book.

We do not know the name of this Sergeant-Major, but Company Sergeant-Major Hart travelled to France in 1926 after the dedication of the war memorials of Arras, Thiepval and Vimy Ridge. His photograph is titled 'Uncle Hart' in my sister Mabel's writing.

THE YOUNGSTER

ALEC RARELY SPOKE OF THE FULL HORRORS of war. Most of the memories of his exploits that he shared with his family were of the lighter side of army life. However there was one incident that he never forgot.

On this occasion the Battalion was just about to go over the top as part of a big attack, when he came upon a young lad, shaking with fright, and almost unable to move. He asked what the problem was and was told that the boy had given a false age, and was only sixteen. And now he wished he was anywhere but at the front under the roar of the guns. This left Alec in a quandary. The boy could not be expected to fight, but if he refused to go over he could be shot for cowardice.

Alec made up his mind and said "You stick to me, and when this is over, I'll make sure you get sent home."

The miserable lad agreed. Alec was known as a lucky bloke, and somehow not only got him safely over the top, but kept him alive throughout that hazardous day. Alec was always fond of the Bairnsfather cartoons, especially, "If you know a better hole go to it!". We wonder whether he found the lad 'a better hole'.

When it was safely over, Alec approached the Senior Officer, who was shocked and after verifying the facts arranged for the boy to be repatriated at the first opportunity. Alec wished him good luck and saw him off, back to headquarters, and then on his way to Blighty.

Alec thought that all would be well with the lad, but heard a week later that part of his journey had to be across a river or canal in a small boat. While they were on the water a stray shell hit the boat. There were no survivors.

CHRISTMAS DINNER 1916

ON DECEMBER 6TH 1916, THE BATTALION made camp on the Maricourt-Suzanne Road. According to the Battalion history[1], heavy rain set in on the 10th. Gum boots and a pair of socks had been issued to each man before going to the front but the muddy condition of the ground was appalling. Two officer and 77 others got stuck in the mud. Three days later an officer and over 70 men were still noted as missing and it was not until the 19th that the bulk of them reported in.

The weather remained villainous and no material was available for shelter. Intercommunication was impossible except at night. Exhaustion set in and 76 men were evacuated to hospital, whilst large numbers were treated by the Battalion Medical Officer.

Frost made a welcome appearance on the 15th so that return to reserve was completed on hard ground, much easier to march on despite the cold. Two Companies were quartered in dugouts near Brigade H.Q. in Mouchoir Copse and in two cellars in Combles. Fires were lit in all dugouts and cellars and the men's sodden clothing was dried.

On December 17th the two companies in dugouts were sent to tents in Maurepas Ravine by motor lorry, but the effects of their terrible experiences were still severely felt, for on the 16th, 17th, and 18th over 70 men were sent to hospital.

The Essex were back in the front line again on the 20th. On Christmas Eve the men marched into camp 107 near Maurepas very tired and wet, and so inauspicious were the surroundings that the usual festivities were postponed, though the Quartermaster provided a pleasant surprise in the form of a free issue of beer.

Working parties were then provided to work at Maurepas, Bray and other places. So depleted was the strength that when the Battalion went to Camp 124 near Sailly-Laurent the total strength was approximately 100 other ranks with transport. The column consisted of Battalion H.Q., two company headquarters, and two Lewis gun hand carts.

The officers celebrated Christmas on January 12th and the other ranks on the 14th. The Battalion continued to feel the effects of exhaustion and weather and there were almost daily transfers to hospital.

This is all recorded in the history of the Essex Regiment and each of these comments was marked with a tick by Alec, presumably to confirm it matched his memory.

He suffered from bronchitis to his dying day but claimed that he was not gassed but that it was the result of standing up to his waist in water in the trenches

It was probably this Christmas that Alec found himself based at H.Q. and so was fed in a mess hut at the base. His platoon had been sent out on patrol, and had spent most of the day in pouring rain and up to their knees in mud. All day long the one thing that had kept the boys going had been looking forward to Christmas dinner. They knew it would not come up to the standard of home cooking, but they all had faith in the cookhouse, that something special would be served up.

When, at last, the boys were served, they couldn't believe their eyes. One partially bad potato to share among each six of them. There was a heated debate as to whether to eat the potato as most of them were ravenous. Alec refused and said they must stand firm. He demanded his right to see the Officer of the Day (O.O.D.). The kitchen staff demurred. They knew they would be in trouble, so they suggested that the boys should leave the mess hut, and they, the cooks would pass on the complaint.

Alec refused. He knew that if they left the table, by the time the officer arrived, a different meal would have replaced the potato. They sat and waited. The O.O.D. came in, preceded by the Sergeant-Major. He barked the order, "Stand to attention when an officer comes in!" They were so tightly packed that standing was impossible.

Alec replied, "Sorry, Sir, King's Regulations Section 28 para 6 subsection (c) – when in dining hall men shall sit at attention at the approach of an officer."

"Is that correct, Sergeant-Major?" asked the officer.

"Regulation 28? Yes, I do believe it says that, Sir" he replied.

"In that case, sit men."

The officer then inspected the offending potato and agreed it was unfit for human consumption. The cook was summoned and told, in no uncertain terms, that a meal was to be provided for the men. The officer was told that the only food left was the cooks own dinner.

"Well, serve that!" was the officer's reply. Alec and the lads eventually got some food to eat and came to the conclusion that for once it had been right to complain.

After the meal one of the lads said: "Wasn't it lucky that Alec remembered Section 28? I could never have quoted it."

"No," said Alec, "it was lucky that neither the officer nor the Sergeant-Major remembered it. I only made it up on the spur of the moment!"

Christmas 1973, Alec sat at the table, surrounded by school children, to eat the traditional school Christmas Dinner. As he was served with the roast turkey with all the trimmings, his eyes filled with tears as he told the children of the Christmas potato. This was to be his last Christmas.

---

[1] J. W. Burrows. The Essex Regiment. Southend-on-Sea: John H. Burrows & Sons, 1927

ALL PALS TOGETHER

POSSIBLY, WITH HINDSIGHT, ONE of the mistakes of war was the formation of 'Pals' Battalions. The great idea was that men would be encouraged to join up if they could go with and stay with their 'Pals' or friends. What was unforeseen was that putting men who lived or worked together in the same group meant that they not only fought together, they also died together. When a Battalion met with disaster, whole streets or villages would be left with blinds drawn, as the telegrams arrived with the bad news.

On one occasion Alec met up with a strange set of 'Pals'. He had been sent to Division H.Q. for some reason and knew he had several hours to waste before his transport back. An officer came up to him and said:-

"Norman, I hear you are a bit of an athlete. Can you play cricket?"

"Well, yes, I suppose so." replied Alec.

"Well, there's a match on and the visitors are a man short. Get yourself over to the pitch."

The pitch was actually a small patch of grass surrounded by huts. Alec reported for duty, and was told to field in the gap between two huts.

"Just stop the ball and throw it to me," said a man whose face seemed oddly familiar. The game started and wickets began to fall. Alec commented on the bowlers luck.

"He's probably the best bowler in England," said his new friend. The next ball was a superb catch. Alec gasped.

"He's always doing that in his county matches," said his friend. "Just a minute," said Alec, "if he plays for his county and the bowler plays for England, who is that?"

Gradually, the whole team were named for him. All were his heroes, but hardly recognizable from the newspaper photos of the time. Alec hardly touched the ball all afternoon, and had no chance to bat. He had, at last, played a game with county players. His one regret was that he did not have the nerve to admit that he had no idea of the name of his new friend, so he never found out whether he was an England player or not.

Obviously, these men were kept together to be used as morale boosters in playing games against men who were temporally 'behind the lines'.

JUST HANGING AROUND

The Battalion was on the move again. This meant that as well as the logistics of moving men and equipment, a new Headquarters had to be set up with communications, both to the front line and Division. Without radio, this meant the laying of miles of telephone cable. Alec and his partner were chosen for the job and set out. Unfortunately, the Essex were not the only ones on the move, as the front line was constantly changing.

Alec thought it best to keep the cable as straight as possible, which meant going straight through a French village. Alec decided to send the cable overhead as this would not only be quicker, but the cable could be hidden among others across the village.

He quickly made the acquaintance of the villagers and got their permission to climb across the rooftops of the houses lining the village street.

They were just going to lay the cable across the roof of the village shop when they heard a noise, and one of the watching men softly called:

"Gardez-vous!"

They looked up and to their horror saw a column of troops marching towards the village, and they were all wearing German helmets! Quick as a flash, Alec and his mate rolled down the roof and came to rest behind the name board of the shop. The French, who had moments before been watching their antics, stood impassively, watching the Germans march through. No-one said a word or gave any indication that the Tommies were there. It took an hour for the column to pass through, while Alec lay, unable to say a word or move a muscle.

Then he got up and finished the job. When his daughters heard the story years later, the only thing that amazed them was that he had been able to stop talking for a whole hour!

Told by his daughter Lilian Thompson.

HANDS UP

ALEC WAS RETURNING TO HEADQUARTERS after mending yet again another break in the wire. He was just about to go through a gap when he heard voices raised in anger. Being cautious, he decided to have a look to see what was going on. He nearly laughed. There was a British Tommy threatening a German soldier with his rifle and shouting, "You're my prisoner!" while the German, also holding a rifle, was obviously trying to make the same point.

Seeing that this could go on forever and not get anywhere, Alec decided to intervene. He stepped through the gap, and pointed his rifle at the German. Seeing that he was outnumbered, the German handed over his rifle and surrendered. They were just sorting out what to do next, when they heard another commotion going on, and through the gap came two more soldiers, arguing as to was the prisoner. The second German was disarmed, and went to join his co-patriot. Alec had just picked up the rifles, when they realised that they could hear two more soldiers coming. The performance was repeated. After this Alec suggested that they should wait to see who else would turn up.

Thirty minutes later the score was twenty German prisoners and twenty-one Tommies to guard them. They decided to shepherd them down to Headquarters to be processed before going on to a prisoner of war (P.O.W.) camp.

As they moved off with Alec and the first Tommy, bringing up the rear, the first lad turned to Alec and said, "I've never been so glad to see anybody in my life. That chap wasn't going to give up easily and I couldn't shoot him as my rifle wasn't loaded!"

"That's funny," said Alec, "neither was mine!"

Between them they had disarmed twenty German soldiers, without a loaded gun between them!

It was, off course, against army regs to have a gun not ready to fire, but a loaded gun was a danger, in spite of the safety catch, if you were walking over rough ground. A slight jolt could accidentally fire the gun, and of course, injuring yourself with your own gun was a Court Martial offence. The Poor Bloody Infantry (known as P.B.I.) was in a no-win situation.

PASSOVER

DRINKING WATER WAS ALWAYS A PROBLEM in the trenches. Each man would have his own water bottle, which would be refilled whenever possible. Water would be brought up the line in 'Jerry-cans' which had previously been used to carry petrol, and no matter how well they were washed out, the flavour would still be there. Sometimes, if the water source was suspect, the water would be treated with chloride of lime, which may have prevented disease, but did nothing for its taste. Sometimes, when conditions were favourable, a dixie of tea would be sent along the line. Although it would start out scalding hot, it would usually be stone cold before it arrived.

With the usual Essex style, Alec's platoon had managed to find a well constructed dug out and improvements were made to make life more comfortable. It was found that a dip in the corrugated roof would collect rain water, which was of a better quality than the official supply. There was even enough for shaving and washing. The Essex had landed on their feet again.

One evening the boys used the water for drinking and washing in the usual manner and after stand down retired into the dug out for the night. It was quiet, there were no alarms, and, tired out, for once they slept well.

The next morning they were roused as usual for stand to and before they had time to start a brew up, an officer arrived to inspect the trench. He admired the dugout and saw the pool of water on its top.

"That's useful," he said and pulling out a mug, proceeded to fill it with water and took a large mouthful. He gasped, grabbed his throat and fell to the ground. Stretcher bearers came at a run and whisked him away, but it was too late to save his life.

Alec reached up, tilted the iron sheet and the water ran off over the edge of the trench. "I don't think we'll use that again" he said.

Soon after, orders were given that stagnant water was not to be used for drinking purposes. It was later believed that gas had been used that night and had settled on the roof, to be dissolved in the water to make a highly poisonous brew. The incredible thing was that the gas cloud had, like the angel of death, passed over the Essex men, safe in their dug-out.

To the end of his life Alec always said that he had never been gassed in the war. He did, however, suffer from chronic chest trouble every winter for the rest of his life. This was eased by the discovery of antibiotics, which would have saved the lives of so many of his fellows.

He died of heart failure following a severe asthma attack in 1973 nearly 50 years after this incident. He was 81 years old.

PASTIMES

THERE WERE MANY PROBLEMS THAT BESET the men in the trenches. Boredom was one of them. In quiet parts of the line men would often be 'standing by' in the trenches With little to do, after their duties, for weeks at a time. Another problem that the Authorities had not exercised their minds on was mental illness. Some men had been accepted into the ranks almost as 'cannon fodder' if they were capable of holding a gun and little else. Others suffered from what would now be termed as 'post traumatic shock' which was then called 'shell shock' or in some cases 'cowardice'. Nobody had the time or inclination to study the effect of conditions or the stress of seeing your friends pulverized, or just the continual deafening sound of the guns had on the men.

It is obvious that there were many men in the trenches who, with proper medical care, should have been invalided out of the army. In his travels up and down the trenches Alec met one of them.

It must be remembered that water was, in some places, a precious commodity and that there was little available for personal hygiene. Alec never knew the name of the man he met sitting on the firing step of a trench, silent and ignored by his fellows. He passed him on a number of occasions and came to the conclusion that he needed no watch or calendar, he could tell the day of the week and the time by looking at the man's face.

Why?

The man spent his weary hours pulling out the whiskers of his beard, one by one, starting at one ear and ending at the other. This would take him a week. Then he would start again as the whiskers would have grown long enough to pull out again. Anyone who knew the situation could look him in the face and by the condition of the beard say, "It must be about 12 o'clock on Wednesday!" and they were usually right!

Which regiment the man belonged to, or why he had not been sent home, Alec never knew. The story only emphasizes the fact that most Generals had no idea of the conditions the men suffered in the trenches at their orders.

OH MY POOR FEET

ONE OF THE HAZARDS OF THE FIGHTING MAN was 'Trench Foot'. This happened when over exposure to cold and wet made the skin turn white and soggy and would then crack open and the feet would become swollen. This, of course, left the feet open to any other infections that abounded in the mire. It was, naturally, against regulations to have this condition, as it would render the soldier unable to march. Some officers, notably Robert Graves, believed that the condition was psychological, rather than being caused by inadequate foot wear.

To try to prevent this, the men were usually provided with a pair of dry socks on going into the trenches, and were told to change and keep their feet dry. Just how they were to do this when, in winter, the water and mud was often over their knees for weeks on end, nobody quite knew. Whole armies of women at home knitted socks as comforts for the troops, some sending them direct to their own 'Tommy'. Often these gifts would have a packet of cigarettes, or, more usefully, a tin of Vaseline tucked in the toe, in the hope that this would be of some help. (To his dying day Alec always had great faith in a tin of Vaseline.)

One day the Battalion was on the move again, a forced march of about twenty miles. One young lad had just had a parcel from home and showed off the offering of his new wife. The first pair of socks she had ever knitted. He decided to wear them for the march. They set off in good style, at the regulation pace, but it soon became evident to Alec that the lad was in trouble. When they had a break, Alec went over to him and asked what was wrong. The lad didn't know, but said, "I can't stand the pain in my feet, Corporal."

"Let's get those boots off, then" said Alec.

With a struggle the boots came off. No sign of trouble . For once the boots were sound.

"Right" said Alec, "let's get the socks off, then."

Off came the socks, and under them the skin was red and sore. The men did not believe it. Then Alec turned the socks inside out. The sole of each sock was a mass of tiny, hard knots. To economise, the young girl had used all the odds and ends of wool she had and had carefully worked the knots to where they wouldn't show. Right under the foot.

Alec quickly twisted each knot until the wool broke, and having removed the knots, told the man to apply some Vaseline before putting them on again. The man did so and the march continued. When they got to their destination and found their billets the men were only to glad to get their boots off. However, when the young lad removed his, the cry of horror brought Alec running. When they looked to see what was wrong, the lad was looking at his new socks, the feet of which had completely unravelled.

"What am I going to do?" he wailed.

"Well," said Alec, "keep the leg parts as wrist warmers and use the wool to pad your toes, and pray that your wife gets some lessons in knitting before making you any more socks!"

BILLETS

THE MEN OF THE ESSEX REGIMENT FOLLOWED a pattern of life that became all too common in the First World War. A period in the trenches would be split into being in the front line; or firing trench, in support, or ready to go forward, or in the third group, the 'reserve'. Being in 'reserve' that although officially one was stood down, the time was spent repairing wire or digging and maintaining trenches. All this was within the sound of gunfire.

This would be followed by a period in billets before being reassigned to where ever they were most needed in the line. This, in the case of the Essex often meant a round trip from Ypres to Arras and back.

Going into billets usually meant a period of regrouping and retraining with a new intake of men to replace the horrific shortages caused by the high casualty rate. Marching with the band, sports days and competitions were arranged to raise morale; and the concert party was usually called on to perform. Frequently malnutrition and exposure (standing up to the waist in water in the trenches) led to minor illnesses becoming major epidemics. One of the new intake at Blangy, near Arras in November 1916 was incubating mumps, which spread through the Battalion like wildfire, causing the whole battalion to be isolated for a month.

One of the joys of Blangy was bathing. In warm weather this could be swimming in the lake, but much preferred were hot baths. Mobile baths were set up and the men could enjoy the luxury of hot water for as long as it would last, whilst their clothing was removed to be steamed, in the hope of deterring lice and fleas.

The greatest joy for some of the men was to find themselves in something that resembled civilisation and the chance to sleep in a BED. It did not occur to some that these beds were rarely cleaned, there were no such thing as sheets, and probably half the army had already slept there.

Alec and his friends knew that there were never enough beds to go round and that the best would be commandeered for the use of the officer. Instead of jostling for one of the few left, they would make straight for the nearest hayloft or barn, where they would find some fresh straw or hay and bed down in comparative comfort.

One day the Sergeant-Major queried their love of the farmyard in an uncomplimentary manner and was told, "That's all right Sarge, we leave the beds for the youngsters. We enjoy the fresh air and are used to it." The Sergeant-Major left, still puzzled.

Alec waited until he was out of earshot before adding the rider, "It may be cold, but there are no bedbugs in new mown hay!"

A LETTER HOME

ALEC'S JOB AS A SIGNALLER GAVE HIM plenty of opportunity to meet lads from other battalions as he passed through the trenches. Often he would meet someone and then not meet up with him for months on end. One such day he came across a lad sitting on the firing step with a pencil and pad in front of him and a worried look on his face.

"What's up lad?" asked Alec.

"Well, it's like this, I want to write home to my missus, but I've never written a letter before."

"Come here" said Alec, "Give me the paper, and tell me what you want to say and I'll show you how to write it."

They settled down and the letter was duly copied and dispatched.

Six months later Alec happened to come across the same group of men again. The young man was again sitting on the firing step, looking at a pad of paper and scratching his head.

"What's the matter with you?" asked Alec.

"I've got to write a letter to the wife" replied the lad.

"But didn't I help you with one last time I saw you?" asked Alec.

"Oh, yes" came the reply, "I've copied it out every week since then" said the lad.

"Well, what's the problem?"

"Look at it" said the lad and he brought out the tattered remains of Alec's original. It had been folded and refolded so often that it had split along the folds and the writing was no longer legible. The poor wife had received the identical letter every week for six months!

Of course Alec gave a hand, but this time he wrote several letters and numbered them so that the poor woman would get a slightly different one each week.

I wonder if she ever found out.

Most letters home were subject to censor by the officer. Many men only sent home field postcards which had standard phrases to be ticked by the sender. These were often issued to troops going into battle to allay worry at home. A few uncensored "green envelopes" were made available. None of Alec's survived.

LIVE AND LET LIVE

FOR ONCE THE ESSEX WERE IN DECENT TRENCHES on a quiet part of the front. Instead of looking out over ravaged no mans land, there were green fields between them and the Jerry lines. All was quiet. Rations were even sent up from the base. Not that they were ever the full complement of food stated in the regulations, more likely what was available at the time.

Alec decided to supplement this. He had recognised the green leaves in front of the trench as potatoes, and he was very partial to new potatoes. It did not take long for him to worm his way out of the trench and to feel his way among the roots until he found large enough potatoes to harvest. Soon he had a hat full, enough for the platoon to have a taste. After tins of bully beef and stew, they were delicious. Soon Alec had a daily job, as soon as they were stood down and the officers had moved off.

One day he took a young rookie, new to the trenches, with him to teach him the skills of scavenging. As they crept over the edge of the trench, the young lad spotted another figure on the opposite side of the field. Quickly he grabbed his rifle.

"Look, a Jerry" he said "I can get him from here!"

Alec grabbed the rifle and put it on the ground.

"Don't you dare," he said "I know he's there and he knows I'm here, and that's the way it'll stay. If you shoot him, there will be six of them ready to shoot us tomorrow, and then there'll be no peace and no potatoes for anyone."

When Alec told this story in later years, he always said that all that mattered was surviving. For him it was a battle against the odds to get himself and his friends back home safely.

In 1972 there was a family reunion and all five of his daughters were together for the wedding of Mary, the youngest. Alec told this story three times to Betty Stigant, his Australian daughter. It obviously held some great significance for him, possibly as the family were all concerned that Australian and American grandsons might be conscripted in the Vietnam War.

I have heard elsewhere a similar story about potatoes. It seems there were other P.B.I. who knew their onions!

THE CELLAR

This story was told by Alec to his niece Elsie Norman.

The terrain of the area around Arras is very varied, the slightly hilly villages of Monchy-le-Preux and Roeux being sited on chalky hills, whist Fampoux is in the valley of the Scarpe, and it's area is noted for its marshy mud. It was here, between Monchy and Fampoux that we found 'Happy Valley' which Alec returned to and photographed in the 1920s and inscribed "200 Essex men drowned in the mud."

We have yet to find the site of the following story but we feel that it is possibly set in the village of Roeux, the scene of much bitter fighting by the Essex boys around the 'Chemical Works'. Roeux still has its factory, but it has been moved up the road. The front line trench ran across what had been the village street, but what was now only a pile of rubble. Things were pretty grim, and if the Germans pushed forward the chances of getting out alive were slim. When Alec was stood down he wandered through the remains of the village, trying to spot the best way out if escape was necessary. As he poked around, he spotted a dark hole beneath a fallen wall. He immediately investigated.

Lighting a match, he looked down and saw what seemed to be a cellar floor. Quickly he lowered himself down, and lit a candle. To his surprise he found, not a store room, but the largest bread oven he had ever seen. This, he realised, had potential. For the next two or three days every spare minute was spent cleaning out his bolt hole and stocking it with spare cans of water. He finished just in time.

The Germans made their advance. At last the order was given to fall back and abandon the village, but it was too late. They were cut off and surrounded. There was no way out. Should they surrender? Just in time Alec said to the officer, "This way, Sir, down here."

In minutes the remnant of the company were sitting on the bread shelves of the bakery. The noise of the battle went on over their heads.

They stayed there for about three days sustained on iron rations and the cans of water. At last it was safe and they returned to join the Battalion after being reported missing. The officer was congratulated for bringing his men back safely. Alec did NOT get mentioned in dispatches !

Later, at a reunion, one young man said that he could not remember Alec, but the one thing he would always remember was sitting in an oven for three days. So Alec said: "Who do you think got it all clean and ready for you then?"

Arras is famous for its 'Boves' or underground caves and tunnels which were dug to mine for chalk and then used for storage. These were used in the First World War to house troops and to transport them to the front. Alec and the Essex lads always included the Town Hall Arras on their reunion trips, and had a yearly reunion dinner on what they called 'Arras Day'. Modern visitors are taken down into the Boves beneath the town hall to see where the troops were stationed. They are always shown wiring put in by signaller-telegraphists. Although this is the work he did, there is no evidence this surviving wiring underneath Arras today was done by Alec!

Monche-le Preux and Roeux are both reputed to have similar caves beneath them

First World War telegraph wiring still to be seen beneath the Town Hall at Arras

THE STARGAZER

ONE OF THE SKILLS IMPARTED TO THE MEN in their many training sessions was that of finding your way about. This seemed fairly simple in daylight, when you could be see of your bearings and landmarks. However, once in the trenches, with a terrain of shell holes all around, it was not so simple. Navigating at night was even more difficult, although the instructor boasted that on a clear night anyone should be able to find their way by the stars. Alec and the others took this lesson to heart, since, having spent most of their lives in the country, they knew the night sky very well indeed.

The night came for them to put their training to the test. The platoon was sent out into No Man's Land. They had to wriggle over the uneven ground towards the enemy lines to gather what information they could find. First they had to find out the condition of the enemy's wire and fortifications, and then if their luck held, to bring back a prisoner for questioning. Alec's group reached their objective fairly quickly, found the required information and got back to their trench without incident.

They went to report their findings, but their superior was nowhere to be found. They waited, puzzled, for him to come in. They had heard no shots or explosions, so where could he be?

He might have fallen or been hurt in a shell hole, so they listened in silence for any calls for help. He could have found a wounded Tommy and be trying to bring him in. They stared out into the blackness, trying to make out any movement, but nothing. They were about to report him missing when there was a movement, and he rolled into the trench.

He passed off his missing hours as having been on watch. Later Alec asked him what had really happened and he had to admit:

"I got over to the trench all right, and tried to get back, but every shell hole looked the same to me, and I was soon going round in circles. I found a trench, but as I could hear no talking, I couldn't tell whether it was ours or Jerry's. I went back across No Man's Land again and found the same thing happened. After spending half the night going backwards and forwards, I crept into a shell hole to rest. As I lay down on my back, I saw the stars and remembered what I had been trying to teach you lot. So I got up again and followed the stars home!"

Alec didn't split on him to the men, and refrained from telling him that everyone else had come home using his method of stargazing!

Alec and his friends had an advantage over most of the others, in that they had lived as small children in London, spent most of their childhood in the country as their parents had moved out of the city, and then spent part of their teenage years in London, either for schooling or when they got their first jobs. This meant that they were at home in the fields and open spaces. And knew how to live off the land, and cope with primitive conditions such as earth closets. When they went to town, they learnt to live by their wits and have quick reactions when dodging traffic and so on.

Most of the war survivors of Pitsea and North Benfleet were lads who had lived in both town and country and had reaped the benefit of both.

THE ORGAN GRINDER

THE ROUTE-MARCH WAS LONG AND HARD. They had left behind the mud and mire of one set of trenches and were being sent to fill the gaps in another sector. At least they were marching on a real road now, one which ran through tiny fields which were still being cultivated.

It was late summer and you could almost imagine that you were back in good old Essex, The only thing to mar the illusion was the tide mark of jettisoned household goods, which showed where tired refugees had dropped what had started out as being treasures and had ended up being encumbrances on their long trek away from the fighting zone. Alec stooped and grabbed an object from the verge. Yes, it was still in working order: an old fashioned French coffee grinder. He turned the handle. The boys laughed.

"Look at Alec," they said "thinks he's an organ grinder. All he needs now is a monkey!" The boys carried on, demanding tunes to sing to and Alec was willing to oblige, even though no music came out. The boys grinned again; Alec was always clowning and thinking up something. No-one noticed that every so often Alec would reach out, grab a handful of something from the field and stuff it into the grinder.

That night they bivouacked in the open. Alec offered to get the fire going for a brew and to get the supper, if his three mates would set up the signal wire and do the other chores that needed doing. They agreed and Alec set to work. To make a decent meal for four out of one tin of bully beef (corned beef) and half a loaf of bread would seem to be impossible for most cooks. An hour later the three came back.

"All right, what's for dinner, then?" they asked.

"How do you fancy Irish Stew with dumplings, then?" They laughed. Another one of Alec's little jokes.

"We're not likely to get that before we get back to Blighty!" said one.

Alec lifted the lid of the dixie. They couldn't believe their eyes. There was stew all right, complete with vegetables, and there, floating on top were four very small dumplings!

No restaurant or home cooking ever tasted as sweet as Alec's Irish Stew. After they had eaten every morsel came the questions.

"How did you do it?"

"Where did those potatoes come from? We haven't had any in the rations for days."

"And the carrots, and the parsnips and turnips?"

Alec laughed. "Look around you" he said. They looked, but could see nothing but green growing crops all round. Alec then explained, "We're camped on a comer between four strips of farm land. This one is potatoes, this one carrots, and here's your parsnips and turnips."

"Cor" said one lad, "I thought vegetables came from the green grocer." None of the had been able to identify the growing crops as a source of food. Then came the final question.

"But how did you manage the dumplings?" they chorused.

"Easy," said Alec, "I just mixed the fat from the bully beef with the flour and put them in to cook."

"But where did you get the flour?"

"What do you think I was doing with that coffee grinder all day? You didn't think I was daft enough to play for your singing, did you?"

MORE TRAINING

Some time in 1916 Alec was sent for further training. One day
there was a pause in the lectures and the men had some free time. Alec
and one of his signaller friends found a quiet comer, where they were
sheltered from the wind by a bank of earth, and started to play one of
their pastime games. This involved timing each other dismantling and
reassembling Morse code tappers. There was a standard time the army
allowed for this and both could manage it easily. To make it more of a
challenge and more fun, they did it first with their hands behind their
backs and then blindfolded.

Unknown to them, one of the examiners was taking a walk along
the top of the grass bank and had stopped above them, watching the
proceedings. When they had both completed this a number of times to
their own satisfaction, the officer made his presence known to them and
asked, "Why are you doing this blindfolded? Surely the regulations don't
require it?"

"No," replied Alec, "but you see, Sir, if one of these things jams, it won't
be on a nice sunny day when we have all the time in the world to put it
right. It will most likely jam when we're up to our eyes in mud, under
fire and a night as black as pitch. And believe me, Sir, no one will light a
lamp for us then!"

"Oh, yes, I see your point" said the officer.

A day or two later the results were posted. As usual, the marks had been
amended to make sure that all the officer' names came first on the list,
but in the next two places were Alec and his friend. They were thrilled,
for they had been told that the ones with top marks would go back to
Blighty for officer training. At last they were on their way.

Chests swollen with pride, they lined up for the announcement at the
passing out parade. The Senior Officer came out with the papers in his
hand for their new postings. Just at that moment there was the roar of a
motor cycle engine. The messenger jumped off and shouted:

"You mustn't give out those orders sir. Read this" and he handed over the dispatch. The officer read it and came back to the men. "I'm sorry" he said "All orders are cancelled. You are to return to your units as quickly as possible. We are expecting another big push at once."

If the dispatch rider had been ten minutes later, the men would have been on the train to Blighty, so Alec missed being an officer by ten minutes!

In a way his sweetheart Florrie was pleased that he never became an officer, as the idea had got around that 'only officer were being killed' because some newspapers printed the officer' names in full whereas 'other ranks' were only referred to in small print. In some places in the trenches, newspapers were delivered, only a day or two old. The *Daily Mail* was delivered to the trenches bearing a story line that our men were quite safe and not being killed. This was meant to allay fears at home, but was inappropriate for the Essex men who had just suffered vicious shelling and had come back from a burial party. The newspaper was dubbed 'The Daily Liar' and all copies were gathered up and ceremoniously burnt on a bonfire.

To his dying day Alec would not have the *Daily Mail* in the house.

Q.E.D.

ONE OF THE COURSES THAT ALEC WENT on, possibly in training to become an N.C.O., contained instructions in not only using a Lewis gun, but how to instruct others in the art.

At the end of the course each of the men had to be tested on how to give a lecture to recruits on one of the subjects they had covered. They were told to prepare a two minute lecture and a demonstration.

When the time came, Alec was given the subject of the Lewis gun, which made him grin, as he was a Signaller, rather than a machine-gunner. However, he took to the stage, and picked up a piece of chalk and approached the blackboard and easel. Without uttering a word, he made a large and very detailed drawing showing all the parts in situ. As this took more than five minutes, there was some muttering from the troops in the audience.

When he was at last satisfied, he turned to the audience, and began his detailed lecture, pointing to the relative parts in his diagram. This took exactly his allotted two minutes. The officer timing him congratulated him on his exact time, and when there were murmurs from the audience, explained that as Alec had not said a word while he was drawing, the time for the diagram was not included. Alec, of course, had read the small print!

The officer then turned to him and said that he should now demonstrate how to strip and reassemble the machine gun. Alec gulped. There was a set time for doing this task, of about two minutes, and Alec knew that this was almost impossible to achieve. He was, after all, a Signaller, not a gunner, and although he was well practised in cleaning his rifle, had little experience of the Lewis gun.

He started the task, with the officer standing over him with the stop watch. He quickly unscrewed all the parts, wiped them and started to reassemble them. He could not believe it. Every screw went in first time. Not one nut, bolt or screw cross threaded, all fell into its allotted place. When he had finished, the officer told him that he had not only done the job within the time limit but he had probably broken the record as well!

His friends asked him how he had managed it and he had to say: "I have no idea. Everything fell into place. The family always said I had a Guardian Angel, but I never expected it to be an expert on machine guns!"

DOUGHNUTS FOR TEA

FOR ONCE THE ESSEX WERE IN RESERVE, behind the lines and in a quiet spot. This meant that although there was little danger from the enemy, there was plenty of danger from the soldiers' real enemy, the Sergeant-Major. They had field day after field day. The sports and tug-of-wars were all right, but one could get heartily sick of route marches, with or without the band, drills, physical jerks and practice trench digging. The lectures might have been interesting if they weren't about subjects that they had already learned by bitter experience. The one really bright spot was when they were allowed enough spare time to explore the local villages.

Very few 'Other Ranks' (O.R.s) had been abroad before, and most had left school with no opportunity to learn a foreign language. It amazed them, that here, within the sound of the guns, and only a few miles from the Front, the typical French village carried on as usual.

When released from duty Alec made his way to the nearest of the villages. Most of the men would make for the local estaminet or bar, but Alec had a strong Nonconformist upbringing, and had 'Signed the Pledge' not to drink alcohol at an early age. All he wanted on an afternoon off was a nice cup of tea and a place to sit down that wasn't ruled by the Army. To his amazement he found it.

There in the village street was a patisserie, which had a small cafe attached. Alec looked through the window to see if they were open for business. His mouth dropped open. There before him was the counter, with Madame behind it. And Madame was standing there piling up mounds of freshly cooked doughnuts on the shelf behind the counter. It was the first time he had seen doughnuts in his three years in France. That decided him. He went in to place his order.

"Bonjour, Mamzell," that bit was easy. "Une cup of tea." If you remembered to pronounce 'tea' as 'tay' you usually got it "and two, deux, what was the word, doughnuts, s'il vous play."

"Pardon, M'sieur?"

"Une tasse du tay and deux doughnuts." The tea was poured and passed across.

"And deux doughnuts."

"Non comprenez."

The conversation went on and got more fraught. There were the doughnuts within sight, but how to get her to understand? After trying all kinds of French words and mime, and being offered everything in the shop, he at last managed to get hold of the coveted doughnuts. He had just sat down, and was about to sink his teeth into his prize, when the door opened and in came another soldier.

"Tasse du tay and deux doughnuts s'il vous play."

Alec grinned. This ought to be fun. It was. It took the man five minutes to explain the word "doughnut" and get served. He turned round and saw Alec grinning and said:

"What's up with you then?"

Alec explained and the man sat down beside him. The door opened again. In came another soldier with the same idea. They watched, and by the time Madame was persuaded to part with two more doughnuts they were both giggling. It was no use, they would have to share the joke.

The cafe filled up, but each soldier had just the same difficulty in getting doughnuts from Madame. The place was beginning to get rowdy with all these mad Englishmen. Madame wondered what was being put in the tea. Then the door crashed open and in came a tiny cockney.

"Ready, lads, here we go again." "Cupper tay and a couple of kill-me-quicks, silver plate, darling." "Oui, M'sieur."

And the lad turned round and carried his cup of tea and two doughnuts back to the only seat left in the cafe. The rest sat there in stunned silence, and then gave him a round of applause.

Seventy years later we told this story to our French friends in Versailles, but they could not identify our doughnuts. However, when we stayed at Pas-en-Artois, which remains undamaged as it was behind the lines, we found a small boulangerie that was selling 'baignelles'. When we bought some, they were indeed doughnuts, stuffed with apple puree. I cannot find the word in the French dictionary, or in Petit Larousse. The latest larger French/English dictionary now lists 'Sorte de Beignet aux Pommes' as an apple fritter, but it is probably the same. We wonder if the doughnut became a local speciality after the first world war!

We also wonder what happened to Alec's rum ration. He was definitely a member of the Band of Hope as a young man, and to his dying day resisted the Demon Drink. It was probably traded for cigarettes, as he was a heavy smoker until he became ill in his 80th year.

CARTON DE WIART

IN COMMON WITH MOST MEMBERS OF THE 'Poor Bloody Infantry' Alec had little time for 'armchair Generals' who were so keen to push men into impossible situations, with little regard for the casualty figures or 'butchers bill.' However there was one man that held the respect of the men and that was General Carton de Wiart. He was known as the soldiers general, and they all knew that he would not order the men to do anything he was not prepared to do himself. He had already lost an arm and an eye, but was still ready to lead from the front.

Thomas Bickerton writes in *The Wartime Experiences of an Ordinary Tommy*[1]: "Our Brigadier was General Carton de Wiart, a Belgian officer who had been wounded seven times. He was a wonderful personality and came up the line in Tommies clothing and went everywhere amongst the soldiers. We all thought the world of him".

One day Alec was at Divisional H.Q. when they saw Carton de Wiart go into one of the huts. Minutes later a stray shell came over and hit the hut, fair and square in the middle. Men ran from all directions to find out what had happened to the old man, most of them thinking that the charmed life was over. As they reached the steps, the remains of the door opened and a very dusty General emerged.

His voice rang out in his famous stutter:-"S-s-sorry l-l-lads I-I-I th-think they've spotted me!"

Siegfried Sassoon summed up Alec's view of armchair Generals with his poem, *The General*[2]:

"Good morning; good-morning!' the General said
When we met him last week on our way to the line.
Now the soldiers he smiled at are most of 'em dead,
And we're cursing his staff for incompetent swine.
'He's a cheery old card,' grunted Harry to Jack
As they slogged up to Arras with rifle and pack.

But he did for them both by his plan of attack."

Carton de Wiart was very different. He went on to command the army in Norway in the Second World War and was then captured by the Italians in time to negotiate their surrender in 1943.

In the words of Carton De Wiart as printed in *The Essex Regiment*[3] by J.W. Burrows:

"My first connection with the 2nd Battalion The Essex Regiment (The Pompadours) was in January 1917, when I was appointed to the commanded of the 12th Brigade, 4th Division, in which the Battalion were serving. For ten months the Battalion served under me and during that period we took part in the big attacks at Arras and Passchendale. The former, so successful and easy on the first day, entailed terrible hardships and losses afterwards, and none suffered more than the Pompadours. Passchendale was very hard from the beginning to the end, and the Battalion had it's full share again of hardships and casualties. But many of the 'ordinary' tours in the trenches entailed just as much fatigue and danger – but less glory!

Never once in all those months did the Battalion fail. It was always a real pleasure to me to go to see men, in the line or out of it, for one knew that they would do whatever they were asked to do, and do it in that cheerful spirit which means so much in war. There were times when it seemed to me that cheerfulness was the greatest military virtue a man could possess. It is almost ridiculous to say so now, but such was the case.

Unfortunately, in war commanders sometimes have to give orders which they know cannot be successfully carried out, but which have to be given to help in some other quarter. This happened, naturally, during our association, but such an order was carried out with the same spirit and ardour as an order which assured an easy success. In my humble opinion, no greater test exists for a soldier.

We had good times and we had bad, very bad times, but the Battalion was always the same and I only hope that some of the members of the Battalion, at any rate, realized how much I appreciated them and admired them for it.

So much depends upon the personal relations existing between men and their commanders, and there has to be much "give and take" on both sides, but with the Pompadours all seemed so easy. I know I always thought I was taking a great deal and giving so little."

It was always very clear from the way that Alec spoke of the General that the men were equally fond of Carton de Wiart, and would have willingly done anything he asked.

According to Burrows in the regimental history, the name Pompadours was awarded to the 2nd Essex Battalion in 1764 when the colour of their coats was changed to Pompadour purple (named after Madame de Pompadour, mistress of Louis XV).

The Battalion lost 1,457 officer and men in the War of 1914-1918.

---

[1] T. Bickerton. Tommy Bickerton Manuscript: Wartime experiences of the ordinary Tommy. London: Imperial War Museum

[2] S. Sasson. . 'The General' from Counter Attack and Other Poems. New York: E.P. Dutton & Company, 1918.

[3] J. W. Burrows. The Essex Regiment. Southend-on-Sea: John H. Burrows & Sons, 1927

ARRAS

ONE OF THE BEST FIRST HAND ACCOUNTS of the battle for Arras is that held by the Imperial War Museum of Thomas Bickerton[1], who was an Lewis gunner with the 2nd Essex Battalion. On the 28th March, Arras Day, his platoon were in the forward line when the Germans made their big push forwards. His platoon stuck to their posts and kept the gun firing until they ran out of ammunition. They fired Very lights to get covering fire from the heavy artillery and received no support as the other guns had been withdrawn when they, too, had used up their ammunition. Bickerton's platoon surrendered after immobilising their gun by jettisoning its firing mechanism. When he reached the German lines he was told that he had held up the German advance by three hours.

Meanwhile Alec was at headquarters in Chili Trench, helping to maintain communications.

According to the Battalion History[2] the bombardment started at 3am, with additional fire from trench mortars at 6am. "At 7am the fire increased [...] Then at 7.15am line after line of the enemy advanced across "No Mans Land" and the ground was thick with field grey uniforms."

"The Essex held on until they were surrounded, for the enemy had broken through our flanks [...] Our orders were to stick to our posts, which we did until we were taken prisoners." The enemy had broken through the unmanned gap, possibly pulverised by the previous bombardment.

A member of 'D' Company is quoted in the battalion history saying; "I noticed the method of the German machine gunners. One man walked in a stooping position with a gun fastened to his back, whilst another rotated and fired. I am sure this accounted for a large number of our casualties"

The main difficulty for the Essex men was the shortage of ammunition. Although messages were sent back for all ammunition to be sent forward, the German advance was so fast that it was impossible to send reinforcements.

"Communication with Battalion Headquarters was severed. The platoons on either flank were overwhelmed after a desperate struggle."

Alec's granddaughter Sally in the Sunken Road held by 32 survivors of the 800 strong Second Essex. General Lundendorf called off his whole 3 week offensive that evening.

By 7.40 the remnants commenced to dribble back. "Reduced almost to a handful-all that remained of the four companies-it was decided to withdraw two men at a time down Chili communication trench... to Battalion H.Q." ..."The H.Q. staff had only just time to escape, leaving a bonfire of papers and maps, for as they left one end of the trench the enemy appeared at the other."

Two cooks, having made the breakfast tea for 'B' Company stopped by their fire long enough to mix chalk and other rubbish with the tea in order that Jerry might have a tasty drop if he reached the spot. Thomas Bickerton heard that "The Germans were cooking breakfast in our Battalion Headquarters." If they drank the tea they were in for a nasty surprise. However if they did stop to cook and eat breakfast, it did help to give H.Q. staff longer to reform.

About 35 survivors from the H.Q. staff, including Alec as a signaller, and others who managed to get out were posted on the sunken road which leads from Fampoux to Gavrelle, where they held the line between the Lancashire Fusiliers and the Machine Gun Corps. The Germans, weighed down with blankets, extra boots, several days rations and quantities of ammunition made slow progress and were only able to advance a distance of less than 2,000 yards. That night the Battalion was moved back to Athies and spent the time transporting ammunition to the front line. On March 30th five officer and 75 other ranks marched out of Athies, the remnant of 500 men. 342 were reported missing, over 80 were later confirmed as killed, the remainder being wounded and taken prisoner.

The site of this battle can easily be found as the Chili Trench Cemetery is today where the old Chili Trench crossed the Sunken Road.

If you climb the banks of the road a clear view is had of the battlefield, with the water tower in sight. The banks made a natural trench and firing step. Now a motorway curves round to accommodate the war graves.

---

[1] T. Bickerton. Tommy Bickerton Manuscript: Wartime experiences of the ordinary Tommy. London: Imperial War Museum.

[2] J. W. Burrows. The Essex Regiment. Southend-on-Sea: John H. Burrows & Sons, 1927

Arras Day veterans & others at Rouex near the sunken road in 1926.

Chili Trench Cemetery

THE SPY

THE 28TH MARCH 1918 WAS ALWAYS REMEMBERED by the Essex boys as Arras Day and for many years after, they had a reunion dinner on the nearest Saturday. Whenever they returned to France, it was always to Arras and its surrounding villages that the boys went.

According to the Battalion history[1]: "The Divisional boundary lay a little south of Gavrelle, where a shallow valley crosses the trench system. The front line trenches at this point were inclined to be swampy, were overlooked by the enemy on Greenland Hill and also commanded by our support trenches and strong-posts. For these reasons and to economise troops, a gap of about 300 yards was left unoccupied, the front trenches being filled in with loose barbed wire."

It is possible that this is the time and place of the following story:

The boys were glad when, at last, they were stood down. The immediate danger was over, but once again the Essex had been left holding the line. After a last look round Alec followed the others into the dugout He put his rifle on the stack inside the doorway, ready to be grabbed if the alarm sounded. In minutes the lads were brewing up, and before long they were drinking a welcome cup of char.

A voice came from the doorway: "Anyone seen Sapper Jones?" The voice belonged to a British officer, but something was not quite right.

"No," replied Alec, "Haven't seen anyone of that name, have we, boys?"

There was a chorus of: "No, Sir, never heard of him." The officer then asked where the first aid post was. This was an odd request, as the post was between them and H.Q.

"Oh, you must have missed it, Sir, it's well camouflaged" replied Alec. The officer settled down for a long chat. He complemented them on the dugout and the well kept trench, and then casually asked them how many gun emplacements there were in this section. The boys raised their eyebrows at this, but Alec was ready with the answer.

78

A R R A S   D I N N E R

    Although a party of us celebrated Arras Day on
the actual ground occupied in 1917 and 1918, a desire
has been expressed that a dinner should be held as
usual.

    This has been arranged for

        SATURDAY, APRIL 24TH, 1937, AT 7 P.M.,

        AT WRIGHT'S RESTAURANT, HIGH STREET,

        COLCHESTER, (OPPOSITE THE TOWN HALL)

        3/6D EACH.

    Major S. Freestone, M.B.E., M.C., will preside.

    There is no need to send money in advance for ticket.
Payment can be made at the dinner.   The important
thing is to let me know as soon as possible - NOT LATER
THAN SATURDAY, APRIL 17TH - if you will be attending.

    A special coach will be run from Bishopsgate, opposite
Dirty Dick's, at 4 p.m., sharp, picking up en route, and
a nominal charge of 1/- per head for those travelling by
this will be made.

    Awaiting your notification.

                J.M. FINN.

205, MAGDALEN STREET,

COLCHESTER.

"Oh, this is the best defended section in the whole front," he said," and so well disguised you could walk right past them without knowing they were there."

Someone cleared his throat nervously. The officer went on chatting. "What troops are in the other end of the trench?"

"I wouldn't really know," said Alec,"but I saw a couple of Lancashires go up yesterday." With that the rest of the lads found their voices.

"I was talking to a couple of Highlanders last night."..."The Gloucesters went up this morning."..."I saw the Suffolks go past."..."The Sunderlands must be there."..."The Devonshires."

Each man named his mates from other regiments. After a while the officer seemed satisfied and took his leave. Alec was the first to grab his rifle and reach the entrance to the dugout. He climbed up and took a careful look around. The others joined him, but of the officer there was no sign.

That night the adjacent trenches were subject to a very heavy bombardment. From the safety of the dugout came the men's voices. "Sounds as if the Lancs have had it!" "Don't think much of the Suffolks chances." "The Sunderlands are getting it."

And so on.

The next day the platoon was withdrawn from the remains of the smashed trenches. As their officer said, no-one could understand how they had survived in an almost undefended trench, with no guns in support, when the empty trenches around them had been pulverised. The men could never admit that a strange officer, possibly a spy, had stood between them and their guns. When the lads asked Alec how he had guessed so quickly, he answered: "Well, have you ever heard a real officer call an Engineer a 'Sapper'. Later, the term 'Sapper' came into general use for the Royal Engineers, from their activities in digging 'Saps' or tunnels in which to lay mines under the enemy line.

Survivors of Arras Day at opening of the Arras memorial in 1932

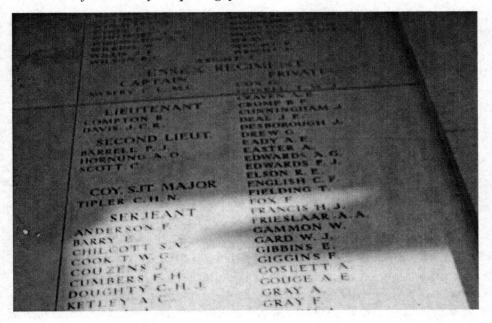

The Menin Gate at Ypres

Alec knew only too well the grave of his closest friend, Signaler Rose, killed by a stray shell with his C.O., Colonel Macculoch, near Arras in 1917. Here around 1962 as another veteran looks on he photographs flowers he has placed on the grave. Below in 1991 his daughter Mary places an Easter candle blessed by M le Cure of Fampoux.

Some modern authors have suggested that stories like this are the product of over-imagination, but Coppard in *With a Machine Gun to Cambrai*[2] writes, "it was not unknown for a German with a good knowledge of English to masquerade as a British officer, enter our own lines at night and get back to his own lines... I remember during the Loos battle seeing a very military looking Major, complete with monocle, and wearing a white collar... I was puzzled about his collar, as all our officer were then wearing khaki collars. Shortly after this there was a scare, and officers dashed about trying to find the gallant Major, but he had vanished."

Alec wasn't the only one 'seeing things'.

Alec and other veterans of 2nd Essex found the names of at least 300 Essex men with no known grave on the memorials at Arras and the Menin Gate at Ypres. At Thiepval on the Somme there are 949.

Above the survivors of Arras Day and others are gathered at the Faubourg d'Amiens Memorial in Arras unveiled on 1st July, 1932 by Lord Trenchard, founder of the R.A.F.

The inscription reads: "Here are recorded the names of 35942 officers and men of the forces of the British Empire who fell in the Battles of Arras or in air operations above the Western Front and who have no known grave."

They include thirteen Victoria Crosses and again over 300 Essex men.

---

[1] J. W. Burrows. The Essex Regiment. Southend-on-Sea: John H. Burrows & Sons, 1927

[2] G. Coppard. With a Machine Gun to Cambrai. London: HMSO, 1969.

THE LADIES OF LILLERS

ON APRIL 12TH 1918, THE ESSEX MEN were being transported by bus or lorry to Busnes, near Lillers, in preparation for an assault on Riez-du-Vinage. This village was slowly being pulverised and was fiercely fought over, as it commanded one of the bridges over the La Bassee Canal (now known as the Aire Canal).

When the conveyance carrying Alec arrived at the market square in Lillers, it was to find that the square was filled with a hysterical crowd of woman and children, who were desperately trying to make their escape and who didn't know where to go or what to do.

Alec realised that it was vital that the transport should get through as quickly as possible but that movement through the crowd was impossible. He stood up and shouted to the women, asking what the trouble was.

"Allemande ici demain," they cried, "Allemande ici demain!"

"Non! Non!" Alec shouted back in his best soldiers French. "Allemande n'est pas ici demain. Ici Essex!" and he pointed to his shoulder flash. The nearest women looked where he was pointing.

"Ah, ici Essex!" they exclaimed, and the shout was repeated throughout the crowd. Minutes later the crowd calmed down and began to disperse, making enough room for the vehicle to pass through. The transport trundled on down the street out of the little town and on into the countryside.

Alec looked round at the lads that he had promised would save the little town. Then he counted up. There were the four friends, who had been through thick and thin together since the beginning. And the rest? About twenty A4s, young men straight from training, on their first trip 'up the line'.

"That's torn it," he said, "there's just four of us to save the situation!" In fact, with the help of the Kings Own, the Essex were to capture Riez-du-Vinage one week later, which probably stopped the German advance on Lillers.

Forty-five years later a party of Essex veterans visited the battlefields and stayed at the Hotel du Commerce, Rue de Gare, Lillers. In the evening the story was told as they were reminiscing. Some of the party thought that it was a tall story, but Madame Croft, the proprietor, joined in. "Oh, yes, "she said, "it is true. I was a young girl in the crowd, and I remember you saying that!"

In 1990 we visited Lillers, but although Mr. and Mrs. John Croft are well remembered, they have, alas, both died, and the Hotel du Commerce is no more.

LA BASSEE CANAL

AFTER LEAVING LILLERS, ALEC AND THE MEN went into trenches near La Bassee Canal, possibly in the Robecq area. Henry Ogle in *The Fateful Battle Line*[1] writes of the area;

'The sphere of operations extended roughly for five kilometres at this time from Robecq in the west to Hinges in the South-east. Robecq, being just over the canal, was shelled regularly at certain times, such as reliefs, but the state of the line when I first saw it would be described as "quiet". In the middle of the sector the canal was in quite a hollow or at least at the foot of a hill called Mont Berenchon. This hollow very frequently smelt of tear gas or phosgene or both and was a place to be crossed with both sped and caution in spite of the quietness of the line."

"Our front line was along the southern edge of the (east-west) ride and this was the road to and through the ruined village of Riez-du-Vinage recently captured. The line straggled through this village and its surrounding cornfields which were soon to ripen in the summer sun."

He continues; 'The German line was no line at all but consisted of holes improvised here and there and held now and then with a few very strongly fortified points with machine guns. They held nooks and corners amongst the ruined buildings and farms and surrounding farms, and no-one knew until we began to probe just where wily Jerry might be, but he could be relied upon to produce a machine gun almost anywhere and to leave snipers about in a puzzling way.'

Riez-du-Vinage would have been about four miles behind the front line at sowing time.

Alec remembered having to get the lads out of the way to let a company of Portuguese troops pass by. Eventually he arrived at H.Q. to find where his platoon should go. The officer looked up and said: "Here's the man you need. Corporal Norman will show you the way."

Alec then discovered that he had been delegated to escort a platoon to the village on the other side of the canal. They moved off and found to their horror that their movements had been seen by the Germans, who opened fire. There was no going back the way they had come. The only shelter was on the other side of a very exposed bridge. Alec looked round to see how many experienced men he had with him. He tried to hide his dismay. The whole platoon were made up of A4s, who had never seen a trench before, let alone had any fighting or preservation skills. There was only one thing to do. He quickly explained the theory of the Indian crawl, which he had perfected in the fields of North Benfleet as a boy.

Keeping their heads well down, the boys wormed their way to the bridge and up onto it. Bullets zinged around them but each one either hit the stonework or the girders and ricocheted around them. Each boy kept his head and kept moving. With surprising speed they reached the other side of the bridge and shelter.

Alec counted them and found that not only were they all present, but they didn't have a scratch between them. If, as we believe, this took place in the fight for Riez-du-Vinage, Alec's platoon were the only ones to cross without casualties.

Henry Ogle of the Kings Own describes his part in the battle vividly;

"My men had been crossing the La Bassee Canal. I had seen them all across the plank bridge under Mont Berenchon and they were climbing up the bank whilst I was still on the bridge. There came a salvo of shells, amongst which sneaked one or two phosgene shells. The men yelled "Gas!" and kept going upwards and therefore out of the dangerous hollow. Just a I stepped off the planks there was a flash and a bang and I felt a sudden wrench across my chest. Down I went and had 1 been on the bridge I would have been knocked into the canal […] How I managed to scramble up the bank I don't know but I got out of the hollow probably without drawing another breath. I escaped drowning, gassing and wounding by shellfire all in one go. The men were delighted with my luck for they liked a 'lucky bloke' to command them."

Thomas Street of Pitsea was almost certainly killed at this time, and has no known grave.

> 2 Argyle Cottages
> Chestnut Rd
> Pitsea. Essex.
>
> May 19th - 1918.
>
> Dear Lce-Cpl. Norman,
>
> We have heard from the War Office That my Son Lce Cpl T. Street. 24430. 2nd Essex Regt B. Coy. 7. Platoon, was reported killed in action on the 21st of April last, could you give me any information, respecting him, or if not, could you ask any of his platoon comrades to let us know about him.
>
> Yours Greatly
> Oblige. Alex Street

He had carried it since 1918. Lance-Corporal Thomas Street was one of the handful of 2nd Essex survivors from 'Arras Day', Good Friday 28th March, 1918.

With reinforcements fresh from England the Battalion went into reserve at Busnet near Lillers for retraining.

On 9th, the Germans launched the battle of the Lys, but were held on the La Bassee Canal. On 18th April, only 21 days after the violent action on Arras Day, the virtually new battalion was sent in to reinforce the Kings Own and to complete the counter-attack which took the tiny village of Riez-du-Vinage.

Sadly Lance Corporal Street was reported 'Missing, believed dead'. He is listed in the memorial at Loos, on the memorial for Pitsea. He was remembered by Alec for 56 years.

In the Second World War the bridges across the canal were held by an 'ad hoc' British and French force for long enough, as Churchill comments, to allow both Alexander and Montgomery with their armies to escape to Dunkirk. The bridges were then blown up to prevent the Germans following them.

Long afterwards a local member of the Dunkirk Association organised a memorial and march past just before we arrived to visit Riez-du-Vinage. He put a notice in the 'Voix du Nord' inviting residents to contact his home address about a return visit by an extraordinary coincidence to our home town of Hastings. He was quite surprised when Alec's daughter knocked on the door to tell him about the defence of the Canal in the first war!

In that war, the Germans attacked from the North during the Battle of the Lys, known to the Belgiums as 4th Ypres. In 1940, they had to force the river from the South, having cut the British Expeditionary Force off from the rest of France. Our old friend, an artillery man, in Fampoux told us his French unit were captured at Lille. They couldn't reach Dunkirk because their guns were horse-drawn.

The bridges were rebuilt after the war, so of course we can't find any sign of Alec's bullets.

---

[1] H. Ogle. The Fateful Battle Line. Edition. Barnsley: L. Cooper, 1993.

THE RUNNER

THE COMPANY HAD MOVED FORWARD. Their main duty was to discover all they could about the enemy strength and depositions. It had soon become evident where the enemy were and that they were there in strength. The Essex men were in a cornfield edging a wood. Unfortunately the Germans had a machine gun in a nearby building which could be brought to bear on the men and regularly swept the field. One man, who was brave enough, had climbed and hidden in a small tree and could observe the gun emplacements, but he could not signal his findings back without either falling out of the tree or betraying his own position to the snipers standing in the corn below.

Somehow the messages had to be relayed, but whenever a man stood, or moved he was peppered with shots from either the machine gun or from the ever present snipers.

Their position was both ridiculous and perilous. They had an observer who could see but not pass on the messages and were in grave danger of being cut off from the support of the rest of the Battalion. In the end Alec volunteered to see what he could do. He wormed his way along the field, beneath the level of the corn until he was out of range of the machine gun. Then, still stooping, he ran as fast as he had ever run until he reached the tree.

He thanked his lucky stars that he had spent so much time on amateur athletics in his youth, and that most of his practice had been on ploughed fields. The soldier thankfully dropped him a note with the bearings of the enemy. Alec took the note and then had to reverse the procedure to get back to the officer. As he wormed his way back he was glad of the games he had played with his dog, Duke, in those fields at North Benfleet. He had always boasted that he and the dog could creep up on anyone unseen, if there was a foot of grass to hide behind. Now it was his own life that was at stake, not the joy of scaring the neighbours.

He had only just got his breath back, when more information was needed, and he set off again. He spent the whole day crawling on his belly or running like a streak of lightning relaying the messages.

The snipers knew that something was happening and kept up sporadic fire in his direction. By the end of the day there was little left of the hedge at the edge of the field and the corn was well and truly trampled. He was one of the few who ended the day without a scratch, but as worn out as if he had run a marathon.

We had wondered where this story took place, as most of the places Alec served in were churned up by shell holes, flood-water and trenches. However, according to *The Fateful Battle Line*[1] by Henry Ogle, Riez-du-Vinage had been four miles behind the enemy lines at seed time and by the time the Kings Own and the Essex boys were fighting there and the corn was beginning to ripen. According to Burrows' history of the 2nd Essex[2] "on the 8th August 1918... the Essex tried another forward movement, but were held up by machine gun fire from houses and snipers posted in the standing corn, 25 casualties being sustained. The following day the line was slightly advanced and then came relief by the 1st Kings Own."

---

[1] H. Ogle. The Fateful Battle Line. Edition. Barnsley: L. Cooper, 1993.

[2] J. W. Burrows. The Essex Regiment. Southend-on-Sea: John H. Burrows & Sons, 1927

'SEND ME BACK TO DEAR OLD BLIGHTY'

ON AUGUST 31ST 1918 THE ESSEX POMPADOURS relieved the Hampshire regiment at Eterpigney. According to the Battalion history[1] the 4th division had been given the task of breaking through the Drecourt-Queant line aside the Arras-Cambrai Road. The advance was planned for the 2nd September 1918.

The night before, the four friends sat talking and the discussion came round to the subject of getting a 'Blighty one'. This was discussed at length, each giving his choice of where he would get a wound that would not be a serious risk to life, but bad enough to win a place on the next boat home.

Several ideas were put forward, some thinking that a leg wound would leave the hands intact for future employment, and some thinking that an arm could be sacrificed. One of the four friends reckoned that the best place for him would be the left arm, as he could then still become a postman if he could walk and use his right arm.

Alec thought carefully and made his choice. As his legs were muscular, the least disabling wound for him would be for a bullet to pass cleanly through the muscle of the calf without touching the bone. That would get him home safely but, he thought, would be the easiest to heal.

Henry Ogle described the battle[2]; 'Men and tanks moved without either hurry or hesitation behind an accurately timed creeping barrage, which only halted at an enemy trench line. The second line offered little more resistance than the first and our line went forward under perfect control, every advance being timed to fit in with the creeping barrage until the tremendous obstacle of the main line was reached.'

John Burrows writes in his history of the 2nd Essex Battalion that: "At 5am on September 2nd the Pompadours essayed a minor operation to enable the Battalion to get square with it's objective and attacked their enemy entrenched on the left of the village of Dury."

Pencilled into the margin of the page of Alec's copy next to this is:

"5.10A.M. ? Wallop Goodbyeee"

Burrows goes on to say: "In the two days operations the Essex sustained considerable losses particularly on the 2nd. There were 24 other ranks killed, 172 wounded and 48 missing."

Alec had got his 'Blighty one' right through the calf as he had wished. And there was his friend nursing a bullet hole through the arm. Today the land rises quickly from Eterpigney to the Drury crossroads, and it was here that the entrenched Germans had mounted their machine guns with perfect sight of the advancing troops.

Alec and his friend helped each other to slap on the standard field dressings. Then they started on the long walk back to the dressing station. Alec always insisted that they walked about two miles using each other as human crutches, and this is a greater distance than from the village to the road. The answer must be that to avoid more damage from the machine gunner, they went off at an angle. They possibly went to the dressing station of the Kings Own Royal Lancaster Regiment who were next in the line.

Henry Ogle wrote;

"Until the passing – it could hardly be called taking – of the second objective, I stood with our Medical Officer, Lieutenant Low, near the first aid dugout entrance which commanded a wonderful view, watching this thrilling and terrible spectacle with feelings I cannot describe."

This was almost certainly the first-aid post Alec made for.

It looks from the letter below as if the Army postal service for the wounded worked very quickly. If the 'Filed Card' gave Florrie official notice of the wound, the 'organised' registered letter must have been sent by a comrade to get there first.

Envelope cover addressed to Cpl A Norman

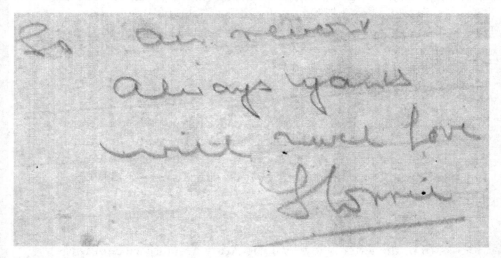

Florrie's letter to Alec

Florrie wrote back to him as follows;

My Dearest Boy,

Many thanks for the Registered Letter and contents I am glad you had it so arranged. I had your field card this morning so now I am looking for a letter. Poor old boy! I am hoping to hear all about it. I also hope they send you home. Buck up, dear! We shall soon be together again. I have had an awful feeling lately. I do not know what they are not going to do and send to us. All sorts of terrible things are suggested.

I have been to the pictures twice also the Hip: this week Going Strong! The Hip ran best I have seen for a very long time. I thought of some of our evenings there. Do you remember several times having seats in the circle? Lets hope you will have many more. I have been having a very busy time lately but now I intend having a good rest. I have no more news only I want you home anyhow. Ma sends her love etc.

So, au revoir. Always yours. With much love, Florrie.

The following letter followed him back to Blighty:

27th Sept. 18
Sig W Bartlett 45212

Dear Alec,

Just a scribble, to let you know how pleased I am that you got to Blighty and getting on quite well. I heard from one of the lads that you were wounded and was walking down. I was looking out for you all day but never saw you, perhaps you went to another divisions aid post. Well Alex as I dare say you have heard our division did extra ordinary well and the prisoners we captured was more than we could deal with at the time, I thought we had captured all of Gerry's armies. I am glad to hear that young Parnell got home too. Is he at the same hospital as you? I am glad to hear that the registered letter was received safe. I was going to write to your home address and tell them it had been sent, but could not get the correct address off anyone. I am writing this in a big sarspa(?) and there's young Phil and Spinks kicking up

H—s delight trying to sing with Humphries joining in with a voice like a trombone. They are all glad to hear you are quite well and wish you a speedy recovery. I dare say you will be having a letter from Phyliss soon as he says he is going to write to you. Well Alex there is very little to write about so I will close with the best of luck.

Yours

W. Bartlett

PS Don't believe all that Bartlett has told you, he is kicking up the hell of a row.

Spinks

PPS Bon chance & best wishes from Lady Phyllis – Will write soon.

This letter makes one wonder whether Parnell was one of the four.

Private W Bartlett was a signaller and also a member of the Pompadours concert party. 'Lady Phyllis' was possibly the stage name of either L/Corporal J. Dick, Private Howard or Private Benson, who starred as well dressed flappers in the concert party. These men were possibly left at H.Q. as it was by then usual to leave a small proportion of each Battalion at base to form the nucleus of a new troop if disaster befell. Bartlett would possibly be on signal duty, whilst others may have been helping the aid post. They were obviously close friends, looking out for one another.

Humphries was the surname of one of Alec and Florrie's bridesmaids but we do not know whether there was any connection.

---

[1] J. W. Burrows. The Essex Regiment. Southend-on-Sea: John H. Burrows & Sons, 1927

[2] H. Ogle. The Fateful Battle Line. Edition. Barnsley: L. Cooper, 1993.

It ain't half cold, Mum!' Concert Party of Alec's comrades in Carnieres,
Christmas Eve, 1918. The writer of the letter, W Bartlett, is in the photo.

BACK TO BLIGHTY

Alec was eventually sent down the line to hospital. As luck would have it, this was the time that the 'Spanish Flu' epidemic was making itself felt. At the time Alec and a friend, possibly Parnell, were at the end of a long ward. Of course Alec was completely immobile and could not get out of bed. He noticed that one man at the end of the ward had become very ill, followed by another four hours later. He kept watch and he was right, four hours later there was another victim. All day and all night he could see this dread disease coming closer. When it was only a couple of beds away he said to his friend:

"The only way to avoid this is to get under the covers and stay there!" They spent the whole night huddled under the covers, wishing they still had their gas masks with them. By the next morning the plague, like the angel of death, had passed over them. They were the only ones in the ward to escape the deadly disease.

One estimate is that world wide between 16 and 17 million were to die from this disease, including about 190,000 allied soldiers and 150,000 British civilians. It must be remembered that both troops and civilians were suffering from the effects of malnutrition after four years of war and had no resistance to this new strain of disease. It is also possible that typhus, septicaemia and a virus similar to the modern day Ebola Disease were responsible for some cases, as the symptoms described by eyewitnesses in *The Roses of No-Mans Land* by Lyn Mcdonald[1] were not all of typical flu.

Eventually Alec and his friend were sent home by boat and were landed at Folkestone. This was followed by several hours of being driven around by ambulance. Alec managed to turn his face towards a window. He could not see much through the slit, but now and again, when the ambulance slowed at a corner, he would get a glimpse of a road name. He got more and more exited. They must be back in Southend for there was Marine Parade, The Esplanade and all the other roads he knew so well. At last they were driven in through the hospital gates, unloaded and taken up to a ward.

The first thing he asked was when would his family and fiancée be able to visit? He was told that travel permits would have to be arranged. He couldn't believe it. Florrie only live a tram ride away in Thorpe Bay and the family were just down the line at Pitsea. The orderly grinned and said "It's still quite a journey to Folkestone!" Alec couldn't believe it, all that journey and hours of being bumped around, and they were still only a mile or two from where they had disembarked. He hadn't realised that every seaside town has a Marine Parade

---

[1] L. Macdonald. The Roses of No Man's Land. London: Penguin Books, 1993.

Alec in 1918 after four years in the trenches.

HOVE, SWEET HOVE

AFTER SOME TIME IN HOSPITAL IN FOLKESTONE, Alec was transferred to convalesce in Hove. The ordinary soldier seemed to think that there was a conspiracy by the powers that be to keep the recovering soldiers at a distance from their families. Alec did, however manage to cross London and get to Pitsea to visit the family and Florrie.

An old photograph has been found in a family collection with Florrie's writing on the back. When it was enlarged on one of the new colour photocopiers, it was recognised by Elsie, who, as child of about three, remembered being visited by a strange man in (hospital) blue who was walking with a stick. This would bear out his story of trying to negotiate an underground escalator and being jostled by a young business man, who said: "Out of my way, man, you are keeping me waiting."

As quick as a flash Alec replied: "Well, you've been keeping me waiting. I've waited four years for you to come out to France to do your bit!"

Alec was also given leave to go to Southend for his wedding to Florrie, which took place on 10th November 1918 at St. Erkenwalds Church. The armistice was signed the next day.

Alec and most of the men based at Hove expected to be discharged at once, as they had signed up for the 'Duration of Hostilities' only, and could see no reason why they should be kept from their families. Unrest swept through the British Army. Those who had survived four years in the trenches had had enough. They all wanted to pack up and go home.

The Government, however, had its own problems. They had promised 'a land fit for heroes', but the peace was fragile and trouble could still erupt. They were also faced with the problem of finding employment for a whole generation of returning troops. They said that the war was not yet over; the enlisted men were not to be discharged.

Trouble did erupt. Christmas came and went. On January 6th the Army 'mutinied'. 10,000 at Folkestone, 2,000 at Dover and 60,000 at other camps all over the country rioted. In some places there was violence.

Five were killed at Kinmel Park, where the red flag was raised, Epsom Police Station was stormed, and the Station Sergeant was killed. Alec always maintained that they did not mutiny, they were, mainly what would be called today 'peaceful demonstrations'. When you consider that these men had all been trained in the art of killing, it becomes obvious that the death toll would have been much higher if the men had really wanted to become vicious!

Alec and the rest of the men who had some mobility decided to take a walk into Brighton. They were a motley crew, with various disabilities, and none of them would ever be fit for a fight. There was Alec's group, ready to slope crutches and walking sticks on command. Behind them came the lorry drivers, all with right arms in a sling, nursing broken wrists, the result of starting handles hitting them when the engines misfired. The blind led the blind. The lame helped the lame.

This was no revolutionary force, it was, to quote Alec, just a group of men who wanted to go home. They marched as smartly as they could through Brighton, being given flags to wave on the way. When they arrived at Brighton they met up with the able-bodied men from Shoreham Camp.

They gathered outside the Town Hall and, according to the *Argus* of the day over 7,000 men were addressed by the Mayor and the Chief Constable[1]. The men sat and sang songs whilst the Mayor (Alderman Cardon) phoned Downing Street to put the men's grievances to his friend in the War Cabinet. He then promised to phone the camps from which the men had come, to arrange for them to have no punishment for their actions, and for a hot meal to be made ready for them. "I'm sorry that there are too many of you to ask to lunch, or I should have been very pleased to entertain you." (It would have been impossible to fit 7,000 into the Town Hall, let alone feed them.) The able-bodied men started their march back to their camps, but those from the nursing homes were incapable of making any further effort.

They decided that the only option was to get to the station and catch a train. It is quite a long walk from Brighton Town Hall to the station, even for a fit person. By the time they got to the station they were all too tired to go any further. They made their way to the platform for the Hove train.

In true British style Authority objected. The man at the gate stopped them and said "Tickets please!" Somehow this did not sound like the riots of the history books.

They ignored the ticket collector and, keeping in formation, marched onto the platform, and formed up 'Entraining files' (lines of six men who would fill one bench on either side of the old style carriages.)

As the train drew in the Station Master bustled up, full of his own importance. "You can't do this" he said and went up to the train engine.

"These men are rioters" he said "I order you not to take this train out."

The engine driver looked at the invalids, drawn up in perfect formation and said nothing. The Sergeant in charge of the men stepped forward and faced his men.

"All trained engine drivers and firemen, two paces, forward march." At once about twenty experienced men stepped forward.

"Well," he said to the driver, "will you drive the train or will we?" The men got their ride home.

Whether their demonstration had any effect or not we do not know, but Alec was sent home to Essex under a 'protection' certificate dated 1st January 1919 and was 'disembodied' on 8th February 1919.

In Brighton Museum is a faded post card showing a proud and portly Station Master standing by a pile of stretchers, waiting to welcome "the gallant wounded heroes" to the town. If it is the same man we wonder why his attitude was so different on this occasion.

The War was not allowed to end officially until August 1921.

---

[1] Brighton Argus, 1918

The wounded heroes with their pride intact

I ENJOYED your supplement celebrating the 125th anniversary of The Argus (The Argus, March 30) but found the omission of one of the most important local stories of the 20th Century lamentable.

I refer to the full-page report in The Argus on January 7, 1919.

Known as the Brighton demob protest, 7,000 services personnel from barracks in Shoreham and convalescents from Hove marched to Brighton Town Hall. The men had signed on "for hostilities only" and felt they should be allowed to go home, as the war had ended.

In other towns, there were riots and in Epsom, a policeman was shot. The government feared revolution.

But this was no revolutionary force – they just wanted to go home.

The 7,000 men sat and sang songs outside the Town Hall. The Mayor, Alderman Carden, phoned Downing Street to put the men's grievances to a friend in the war Cabinet. He also phoned the camps to insist the men were not punished and would be served a hot meal on their return. He apologised for not feeding them himself, regretting that he did not have room for them in the Town Hall.

His sensible actions defused a difficult situation.

At the time, The Argus did not print the rest of the story but my father told me what happened.

The men decided to get a train back to Hove and Shoreham. When they got to the station, they were met at the gate by a ticket collector who said "Tickets, please!". But he was ignored and the men went on to the platform, where they lined up in "entraining order" – lines of six, to fit into the individual carriage layout.

As the train arrived, so did the stationmaster, who told the train driver: "You can't take these men, they are rioters and have no tickets."

A demobbed sergeant then stepped forward and addressed his fellow soldiers: "All train drivers and firemen, two paces forward-march!"

About 20 experienced railwaymen stepped forward. "Well," he said to the driver, "will you drive the train or will we?"

The men got their train and most were sent home within weeks.

Brighton Museum contains a faded photo of the stationmaster standing by a pile of stretchers waiting to welcome "the gallant wounded heroes" to the town. I wonder if it was the same man.

Mary Cole
Anglesea Terrace,
St Leonards-on-Sea

'The wounded heroes with their pride intact' Brighton Argus, 26th April 2005

THE CROFTS OF LILLERS

AT THE END OF THE FIRST WORLD WAR A YOUNG GIRL married a British Soldier, John Croft and settled in Lillers and ran the Hotel du Commerce, Rue de Gare. After the war, Essex veterans regularly went back to France to visit the graves of lost comrades, and during those visits Alec befriended the Crofts, who provided him with many favourite anecdotes, this time about their exploits in the Second World War. In 1939-40 John was interned, leaving his wife to carry on the business. The Hotel was the most convenient in the town, being opposite the station, and was quickly requisitioned for the use of a German officer. Then began a game of cat and mouse that was to last the length of the war, for Madame Croft was a leading member of the Resistance, and her Hotel was also convenient for escaping service men, who could be smuggled on and off trains.

She told many stories of her experiences. On one occasion, the German officer demanded that she should make him a twelve egg omelette for his supper. As food was in short supply, she was loathe to do this, but did have the eggs that were issued for his use. She went into the kitchen, leaving the door open, and began breaking the eggs into the bowl. The Germans heard the crack and then the plop as each egg went into the bowl. They counted one, two, three,... eleven, twelve, and then cheered. Madame continued to make the omelette and served the huge offering to the officer. Then she retired to the kitchen to make another omelette for the six British Servicemen who were hiding there. The Germans may have counted the eggs, but it did not occur to any of them to count the mixing bowls!

On another occasion, she was returning from the market when she was stopped by a patrol, who insisted on searching her. She uncovered her basket to show that it was full of vegetables. When the soldier went to investigate further, she berated him, saying that these were for the Commandants lunch, and if he bruised or damaged them he would be on a charge. The soldier let her pass, and as soon as she got back to her kitchen, she unpacked her basket, took out a revolver from the bottom and said to a waiting friend "Be careful where you hide that!" Another time she had to stand by, showing no emotion, as one of her friends

The Crofts of Lillers outside the Hotel du Commerce, Lillers

was dragged away, beaten and arms broken, knowing that if she showed that she knew this man the lives of all the resistance workers and her escaping boys were at risk.

The Germans obviously suspected that something was going on in the hotel, for one day they turned up in force to search for money, papers and anything else that might implicate the resistance. Madame readily agreed, with the proviso that her elderly Mother should be got out of bed first, as the shock of having her room searched might be too much for her. The officer agreed to wait until the old lady was ready. Madame gave orders to a little serving girl in the local patois. The rooms were all searched, leaving Grandmere till last. When the soldiers entered the room, they were confronted by an extremely fat old lady wedged into an armchair. They quickly stripped the room, searching every inch of it and every movement watched by the old lady. At last they had finished and left, with all the staff smiling sweetly at them. Madame hurried upstairs to Mama. Mama greeted her with:

"Get me back to bed. And next time you want me to sit on something, give me another cushion!" All the evidence the Germans needed to

Lillers now boasts a new memorial, near to the war memorials, dedicated to the resistance workers of the town.

close down the group was safe under her cushion, and not one of the soldiers had dared to suggest that the old lady was moved, and none of the soldiers understood the orders given in patois!

In 1961 a group of Old Soldiers from Essex stayed at the Hotel. When they were swopping stories in the bar, Alec told them his "ICI ESSEX" yarn. Some of the boys felt that it was a tall story, but Madame said "Oh, no, that is true, I remember you. I was one of the girls in the crowd." At that time the BBC was broadcasting a series based on the escape routes used by crashed air-force personnel. Alec asked Madame how accurate this was and Madame told them that an escape committee consisted of as few people as possible. In Lillers the essential people besides herself were:

The Doctor, in case people were wounded. The Town clerk, to provide documents. The Grocer, to fiddle the ration cards to feed them. The Tailor, to alter clothes so that they could pass unnoticed.

Later that night, two men came in and quietly sat down in the bar for their drink. Alec watched them. They were joined by another man. Alec turned to Madame and said:

"Is that the Doctor and the Clerk?" "Yes," said Madame.

"And is that the Tailor, just come in?"

The door opened and another man of about the same age came in.

"And I suppose this is the Grocer, then?"

"But of course" said Madame.

Twenty years on, the resistance team were still meeting every night for a drink at the Hotel du Commerce.

Unfortunately by the time we visited Lillers the Crofts were dead and the Hotel closed, although Madame's daughter still lives in the town.

Lillers Market Place c1962 when Alec and the 2nd Essex visited John Croft

EPILOGUE

ALEC MARRIED FLORRIE ON 10TH NOVEMBER 1918 at St. Erkenwalds Church, Southend. The Armistice was signed the next day, which gave rise to the family joke that for the world the war ended on 11th day of 11th month 1918, but for the Norman family it was the day it all began. However Alec and Florrie had a happy life together.

When Alec was fit enough, he returned to work for the General Post Office (G.P.O.) as a linesman. To his disgust, he found that no-one appreciated his four years of signaller experience and that jobs had been reserved for those that had been conscripted rather than those that had volunteered. This meant that he had to compete for his own job and no concessions were made for his experience. This was to prove to be fatal. He was horrified by the lack of leadership and safety precautions. He tried to explain the difficulty to those in authority and to say that, if he were given seniority, he would see that the crew were properly trained. This was refused, and when his father-in-law, Henry Early, offered him a job in his tie factory, he accepted, as he could no longer stand by waiting for an accident to happen.

The week after he started his new job, his old crew went out after dark to repair a telephone line. They parked their lorry on a sharp bend in the road, lowered the tailboard so that it covered their lights and started work. They had no lookouts. A lorry speeding round the bend on what should have been an empty road ploughed into them. All were killed. A week later the G.P.O. offered him a supervisors job, but Alec would not let down his father-in-law.

In the 1920s and 30s Alec and Florrie ran a haberdashery shop in Langdon Hills (now part of Basildon). While running the shop they both became involved in the Boy Scout organisation, with Florrie starting the first Girl Guide Company in the area. For this she even had to make all the uniforms on her own sewing machine.

It was hard to make a living during the depression and Alec started a delivery round for the Tilbury Laundry. In 1936 it was decided to close the shop and move to Worthing Road where there would be enough room to continue with the laundry business.

Florrie Norman on her wedding day

In 1937 they made another trip to France, for Alec had won first prize in the 'John Bull' bullets competition. His slogan was 'Football Fans – Roaring Lions envying Giraffes'. This won £600 which was enough to buy their home, 'Bangalore', and one of his rare holidays.

On this trip, Florrie, pregnant again for the fifth time, purchased a length of old, fine nuns veiling to make a Christening gown for the new arrival. The dress was duly made and worn, but a few years later, when the country was once again at war, it was cut up to make confirmation veils for two of the neighbours children. In 1978 the material was reworked to become the christening gown of the youngest of all the 15 grandchildren. Neither Alec or Florrie were alive to see it.

On 3rd of September, 1939 the family gathered around the wireless set. Betty was told to take Mary, the youngest out to play in the garden. Betty was seven years old and Mary not quite two. The Prime Minister spoke, and said the fatal words "we are now at war with Germany". There was silence and then, remembering all her friends who did not come back, Florrie said: "Thank God I didn't have boys!" Little did she know that her eldest daughter, Mabel would volunteer as a nurse for the V.A.D. and end the war in Ceylon, nursing members of the forces with infectious fevers!

According to Beryl, who was about twelve at the time, Alec went rushing out to volunteer to join the forces, thinking his experience could be useful, but at 46 years old and bearing the scars of his war wound, he was told he was too old for active service, and so volunteered to become an Air Raid Precaution Warden, which he could do whilst working at a tie factory.

However amongst his papers we found a warrant card stating that he had signed to become an A.R.P. Warden in April 1939. We do know that he was attending 'civil defence' talks in Brentwood at about that time. We now believe that this was in connection with Churchill's 'Underground Heroes' who were experienced ex-soldiers, and those to be trained to act as saboteurs in case of invasion by the Germans. He is known to have a box of ammunitions buried beneath his allotment (I remember as a chid being told to keep away from his overgrown rubbish heap) and a collection of glass bottles in his shed for the manufacture of Molotov cocktails. He also had a hand written note book on the use of various grenades and so on. A far cry from the accepted role of shouting "Put that light out!"

This came to nothing, for in December 1940 he was called out to inspect an unexploded bomb. He and a fellow warden by the name of Clements were inspecting the crater when the bomb exploded. Alec was thrown up into the air, over the top of a poplar tree. He recalled thinking, firstly, "I am dead and on my way to heaven" and then, as he began to come down, "I hope this mud lands before me and not on top of me!"

Mr Clements was blown a similar distance, but sideways. They met, crawling along, both looking for the body of the other. At the hospital everyone thought he was dreaming and would not believe that he could be thrown so high and live to tell the tale, but neighbours, who knew he had gone to look for the bomb, were up on a roof mending bomb damage, heard the blast, looked up and saw him fly over the tree. They were convinced that he had not survived. When a note in the National Papers reported that the two wardens were in Billericay Hospital, his niece visited him. When asked how she knew it would be him, she replied:-
"It had to be you, to do that and survive. The family always said you had a guardian angel!" The main damage was, once again, to his leg and the

Card to Alec from France, 1963

surgeon was so surprised by the amount of shrapnel that he removed that it was brought in on a dinner plate to be displayed in the ward.

After the war Alec worked full time as a tie cutter, the skill his father-in-law had given him, until the depression of the 1950s made life difficult. In 1953 he was given a job at Rotary Hoes, firstly as a mechanic in the experimental department, and later, when he had proved his skills, assembling hydraulic pumps. It was his proud boast that even after his retirement the repair shop was finding that pumps he had assembled never seemed to need repair.

Florrie became a local Councillor after the war and was in great demand for Health and Education Committees. She was made a Justice of the Peace and was well known for her work in the Juvenile Courts.

During the years between the wars an 'Old Boys' organisation was formed for the survivors of the Essex Regiment. The moving spirit of this was Jack Finn of Colchester, who kept in touch with as many of

Lance-Corporal Jack Finn, Military Medal, at home and in the Christmas 1918 concert party

the 'Boys' as possible. He organised annual 'Arras Day Dinners' between 18th–28th March, usually in the Chelmsford Area. Trips were arranged back to the battlefields; the first was possibly after the opening of Thiepval, Arras and Vimy Ridge Memorials. Photographs still exist of these early visits and they were continued regularly in peacetime until the 1960s.

Florrie and Alec joined several of Jack Finn's trips to France and when Alec retired they both went for a trip to see the new grandchildren in America, crossing in style on both the Queen Mary and the Queen Elizabeth. A month after their return Florrie died of heart failure and Alec did not go to France that year.

The next year Alec set out once again with Jack Finn and a much smaller party of Essex men. It was not the same. The French Autoroute system had caught up with the battle fields. Although the French had been careful to avoid the Cemeteries, they were in close proximity. At Pont du Jour, where Signaller Rose is buried, there is no longer the roar of guns. The roar of traffic has taken its place. When he came back he said: "That's it. We won't be going again. They've built a motorway across our valley." They made the decision not to return but to keep their memories as they were.

All but one kept to this. Jack Finn's family packed him up and sent him on an old age pensioners' holiday. They saw him off on the coach to Folkestone and phoned the Hotel the next day to find if he had settled

Alec writes 'Muddy Road on way to Happy Valley. 200 Essex Soldiers were drowned in the mud'.

Happy Valley cemetery

in. They were horrified to discover that he had paid his bill and signed out. They waited anxiously for a week to hear from him. Then the coach arrived back with the pensioners and Jack got off the coach. When they asked him where he had been, he said the temptation of the ferryboats had been too much and he had been across to France to say his last goodbyes to the 'Lads'.

It took me another thirty years to find 'our valley'. The clue came with a sign post at Monchy-le-Prieux pointing to 'Happy Valley Cemetery'. We went down the 'muddy road' and started to recognise the photos of the 1920s. We stood where he must have stood, helpless, when the 200 Essex men drowned in the mud. In a way we were glad he was not with us, for when we walked under the motorway, we found that 'Windmill Hill', the site of the German machine guns, had been sliced in half to make for the T.G.V. to link Paris with the channel tunnel.

While digging this stretch of line, the remains of a large number of soldiers were found but, alas, they could not be identified as Alec's missing 200. The local people say that to this day the "muddy road" still gets flooded in winter!

Alec continued to live in Laindon until I married in 1972, although this too, was undergoing change in the building of Basildon New Town. In 1973 he came to live with us in St. Leonards, Sussex, but as he left Essex his health began to fail. He determinedly lived to see his youngest grandson born, but ten months later, like all old soldiers, he just 'faded away'.